The
Boy
and
the
Dog

The
Boy
and
the
Dog

SEISHU
HASE

TRANSLATED FROM THE JAPANESE

BY ALISON WATTS

SCRIBNER

LONDON NEWYORK SYDNEY TORONTO NEWDELHI

First published in the United States by Viking,
an imprint of Penguin Random House LLC, 2022

First published in Great Britain by Scribner,
an imprint of Simon & Schuster UK Ltd, 2022

1 3 5 7 9 10 8 6 4 2

Simon & Schuster UK Ltd
1st Floor
222 Gray's Inn Road
London WC1X 8HB

www.simonandschuster.co.uk
www.simonandschuster.com.au
www.simonandschuster.co.in

Simon & Schuster Australia, Sydney
Simon & Schuster India, New Delhi

A CIP catalogue record for this book is available from the British Library

Hardback ISBN: 978-1-3985-1538-3
eBook ISBN: 978-1-3985-1539-0
eAudio ISBN: 978-1-3985-2033-2

Illustrations by Tatsuro Kiuchi
Book design and map by Lucia Bernard

Printed in the UK by CPI Group (UK) Ltd, Croydon, CR0 4YY

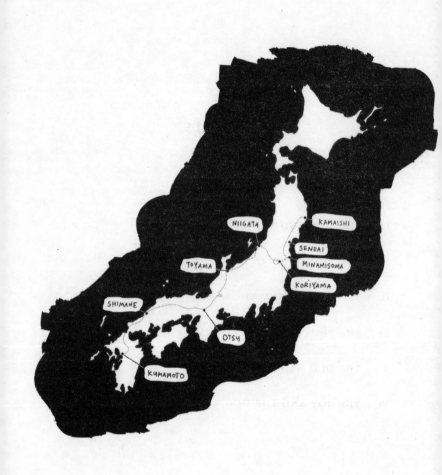

Contents

i

The Man
and the Dog

1

There was a dog in the corner of the convenience store parking lot. It had a collar but no leash. It was skinny but looked alert. Maybe the owner was inside the store. Maybe the dog belonged to a disaster victim. Such were Kazumasa Nakagaki's thoughts as he parked his car.

Six months had passed since the triple disaster of earthquake, tsunami, and nuclear meltdown. There were still people living in evacuation shelters. Some also slept in their cars, because pets weren't allowed in the shelters.

Kazumasa went into the store to get coffee, cigarettes, and a sweet roll. After making his purchases and dispensing coffee from the self-service machine, he went outside to the ashtray stand and lit up a cigarette. He removed the wrapper from his roll and chomped on it between puffs of his cigarette.

The dog was still there. Staring at Kazumasa.

"That's weird . . ." Kazumasa wrinkled his brow. He had not seen anyone else in the store. Plus the only car in the parking lot was his.

"Your owner in the bathroom?" Kazumasa said to the dog. In response it edged closer.

It looked to him like a German shepherd mix. Shepherd in appearance but slightly smaller, with a long nose and ears.

The dog came over to Kazumasa and stopped in front of him. It pointed its nose up and sniffed the air. Obviously it was not interested in the cigarette.

"You after this?" Kazumasa waved the sweet roll over the dog's head. Drool trickled from its mouth.

"Hungry, buddy?" He broke off a corner of the roll, placed it on his palm, and brought his hand down to the dog's mouth. The dog took its time to sniff at the bread before eating it.

"So that's it. You're hungry. Wait a sec."

Kazumasa stubbed out his cigarette, placed his coffee cup on the ashtray stand, and crammed the rest of the roll into his mouth in one bite. He went back into the store and selected a dog treat labeled chicken breast jerky. From outside, the dog's eyes tracked his every movement through the window.

"That dog belong to anybody?" Kazumasa asked the cashier. The cashier glanced out the window and turned back with a bored expression.

"It's been there all morning. I'm thinking of calling Public Health."

"Oh, gotcha."

Kazumasa took the jerky back out to the ashtray stand. The dog wagged its tail.

"Here you go, get this in you." Kazumasa tore open the packet and offered the dog a stick of jerky. The dog wolfed it down. Then another piece. And another. Finally the last stick. In no time the jerky was all gone.

"You were really hungry, buddy."

Kazumasa reached out to pat the dog's head. The dog observed him. It was being neither friendly nor wary.

"Let's see this." Kazumasa examined the dog's collar. It was leather with an engraved tag attached.

"Tamon? Is that your name? Kinda unusual."

He'd expected the tag to have the owner's address or telephone number, but there was only the dog's name.

Kazumasa lit another cigarette and sipped his coffee. The dog—Tamon—stayed beside him. It wasn't begging for food or asking to be petted but was simply being there, at Kazumasa's side. Almost as if it thought that was the polite thing do in return for the jerky.

"I gotta get going," Kazumasa informed Tamon when he'd finished smoking. He was on work time and had stopped off at the convenience store only because he wanted a snack. After the disasters, the seafood-processing factory where Kazumasa used to work had gone bankrupt. He'd lived off his meager savings until finally landing this job. He couldn't afford to get fired.

Kazumasa got in his car and set down his coffee in the cup holder. He started the engine and shifted into reverse.

Tamon stayed next to the ashtray. Motionless. Staring at him.

In his head, Kazumasa heard the cashier's voice: *I'm thinking of calling Public Health.*

What'll happen to it if the authorities take it away? The instant this thought entered Kazumasa's head, he leaned over and opened the passenger-side door.

"Hop in," he called.

Tamon came racing over and leapt up onto the front seat.

"Keep still. And don't piss inside the car."

Tamon lay down on the seat, looking as if he had been riding there all his life.

"HEY, WHAT'S A DOG doing in there?" Numaguchi looked suspiciously over at the passenger seat as he counted the money.

Tamon looked at Kazumasa.

"It's my new dog," responded Kazumasa.

"Didn't know you had enough cash to spare for a dog." Numaguchi put the money back in the envelope and stuck a cigarette in his mouth. Kazumasa promptly offered a lighter.

Numaguchi had been ahead of Kazumasa in high school.

He'd always had a bad-boy reputation and had drifted into the Sendai underworld after leaving school, without ever getting a regular job. Though he had not been formally inducted into any yakuza gang, he behaved as if he was a member. His current gig was the resale of stolen goods.

When Kazumasa's savings had almost run out, he went crawling to Numaguchi, who gave him a job as a delivery driver.

"Yeah, um, it's complicated," Kazumasa hedged. If he let slip that he'd picked up the dog while out on a delivery, it was a sure bet he'd cop a fist straight to the mouth.

"I s'pose it's only been six months. Must be people who can't look after their pooches anymore," Numaguchi mused, swiveling his head as he blew smoke rings.

They were in a corner of the warehouse district near Sendai Airport. The Pacific Ocean was visible to the east. Before the disasters, the area had bristled with all kinds of storage facilities, which had been inundated by the tsunami.

"This place is better than it was six months ago, but it's still not back to what it was by a long shot."

The city had managed to repair the sunken, buckled, and debris-strewn roads, but otherwise not much progress had been made in rebuilding. Numaguchi rented out a warehouse from a transport company. According to him, the company got into trouble when work dried up, so he'd gone to them and negotiated to rent it for a song.

"See if you can train it to bark when cops get close," Numa-guchi said.

"Dunno if I can."

"Course you can. Dogs are supposed to be smart."

"Okay, I'll give it a go."

"Yeah, do that. And hey, I got a favor to ask."

"What?"

"Want some more work? Money's good. You used to race go-karts at the SUGO track, right?"

"When I was a kid," Kazumasa replied. It was true that up to the end of junior high he used to head over to the track every weekend to drive go-karts. He had dreamed of being an F1 driver. But then he realized his talent wasn't anything out of the ordinary and gave up. That had been in his third and last year of junior high.

"Well, you still got the knack, and Suzuki was pretty impressed the other day. You drove him, right?"

"Yeah."

Suzuki was like a sworn brother to Numaguchi. Two weeks earlier Kazumasa had driven him from the warehouse to Sendai Station.

"He said your acceleration and cornering were so smooth it was like being in a Rolls-Royce instead of an old bomb."

Kazumasa scratched his head. He didn't know how to reply.

"You sure can drive, and not just a go-kart."

"I suppose my driving's a bit better than average."

"Yeah. So how about doing something with it?"

"Whaddaya got in mind?"

Numaguchi flicked away his burned-down cigarette. "So I was asked to provide assistance to some foreigners, like, a gang of thieves. More an order, you could say. Can't say no."

"A gang of foreign thieves?"

"Dickhead. Keep your voice down."

Kazumasa covered his mouth after receiving a slap upside the head.

"Your job would be to drive them back to their hideout after a heist."

Kazumasa licked his lips. Delivering stolen goods was one thing—in a pinch, he could claim ignorance—but driving around thieves who'd just committed a crime was a different story. If caught, he'd be treated as an accomplice.

"It pays good." Numaguchi rubbed together his right index finger and thumb. Kazumasa looked at the circle Numaguchi's fingers made and saw in it the faces of his mother and sister.

"Can I think about it?"

"Okay, but I gotta know soon. Give me an answer this week."

"You bet."

Kazumasa shifted his gaze from Numaguchi to the car. He saw Tamon inside, still as a statue, staring at him.

2

Kazumasa poured some of the dog food he'd bought at the home goods store into a ramen bowl and placed it in front of Tamon. The dog began wolfing it down noisily.

"You really are hungry, buddy. There's no meat on you at all."

Kazumasa sat cross-legged on the tatami floor, smoking a cigarette as he watched Tamon eat. In the car he had leaned over to pet Tamon in the passenger seat every time they stopped at a traffic light. Tamon's body was gaunt beneath his fur. His ribs stuck out, and he had scabs all over his body.

"Where the hell did you spring from, buddy?"

Tamon finished his meal, licked his chops, and sat on the tatami.

"C'mere."

Tamon moved closer to Kazumasa. His eyes narrowed in satisfaction when Kazumasa stroked his head and chest. Kazumasa had never had a dog before, nor had he wanted one, but this wasn't half bad, he thought.

His cell phone rang. The call was from his older sister, Mayumi.

"What's up?" he answered.

"Nothing much, just wondering what you're up to."

He could tell straightaway that Mayumi was lying. She was probably worn out from caring for their mother and had called to vent but changed her mind when she heard Kazumasa's voice.

"Anything happen with Mom?"

"Nothing in particular, but . . ." Her voice trailed off and ended in a sigh.

Last spring their mother had begun showing signs of early-onset dementia. For a while her symptoms were relatively mild, but they worsened when she was living in the emergency evacuation shelter after the disasters. The strain of leaving her familiar home environment and having to endure communal life with large numbers of people was too much for her. It had taken two months before her house was cleaned up, repaired, and fit to live in again.

Mayumi used to have an apartment in town but had let it go in order to move back into the family home after the tsunami. She could not bear to stand by and watch while their mother went downhill and struggled on her own. But it was a constant mental strain. Mayumi was getting thin and worn out. She was in her thirties—the prime of her life—but she often looked prematurely middle-aged.

"Geez, I'm sorry, Mayumi. If I wasn't so useless I could help make things a bit easier for you moneywise."

"It's the times. Don't take it to heart."

"Yeah, but . . . Oh, by the way, I picked up a dog."

"A dog?"

"Yeah. I think he might've lost his owner in the disasters. But he's well-behaved and smart, so I'm keeping him. Next time I come over I'll bring him with me. Dogs are supposed to be good therapy for sick and old people, aren't they? And dementia patients. They make them calmer."

"Yeah, I've heard that too. Bring it. Mom would love that. She always wanted a dog."

"Mom wanted a dog?"

"Yeah, she did. Her family had one when she was a kid. But Dad didn't like animals, so he never allowed it."

"First I've heard of that."

"It was before you were born. Mom was disappointed, but she found out you were in her tummy not long after and forgot about the dog."

"Uh-huh."

"What's the dog called?"

"Tamon," Kazumasa replied. He was glad to hear a bit of life return to Mayumi's voice.

"What kind of name is that? It's a bit weird, isn't it?"

"That's what the tag on his collar says. I think it's Tamon after Tamonten—you know, the guardian deity."

"Whatever. Anyway, bring him around as soon as you can. I haven't seen Mom smile in months."

"Sure thing. Will do."

"Ah, I'm glad I called. Talking to you has made me feel better than I have in a while. Thank goodness for family," Mayumi said before hanging up.

Tamon was asleep with his jaw resting on Kazumasa's thigh. He seemed to trust Kazumasa, his sleeping face calm and his back rising and falling rhythmically. Gently, so as not to wake him, Kazumasa placed his hand on Tamon's back. The warmth traveled up his arm and crept into his heart.

3

Kazumasa searched the internet for anything he could find about Tamon. He tried every keyword he could think of: Tamon, dog, male, German shepherd, mixed breed, missing, disasters. But he came up with zilch, not a single hit. Apparently nobody was searching for Tamon. The owner was either dead or had suffered so badly in the disasters that he or she was in no position to look after a dog. In any case, it put Kazumasa's mind at ease about keeping him.

Kazumasa put Tamon in the car, and they set off to see his mother. No time like the present. It had been only yesterday that he'd spoken to Mayumi, but sooner was better than later.

The family home was a freestanding house in a residential area south of the Natori River. Kazumasa's father had taken out a loan to buy it soon after Mayumi was born. After his death, they had paid it off with what remained of his life insurance policy. Kazumasa and Mayumi had talked about selling the house when their mother's dementia became so bad that they needed to put her in an institution, but that idea had faded since the disasters.

The house stood on a narrow plot with only enough yard for a flower bed and one parking space. Kazumasa left his car parked in front of Mayumi's small one. It was jutting out into the road, but the neighbors never complained.

"Let's go, Tamon. Be on your best behavior."

Kazumasa attached the new leash and collar he'd bought and took Tamon out of the car. He opened the front door and called to Mayumi. "It's me. I brought Tamon."

Her answer came after a beat. "Kazumasa? You with the dog?"

"Sure am." Kazumasa wiped Tamon's feet with the damp towel he'd brought. He removed his own shoes and stepped up over the threshold into the house. Mayumi emerged from the bathroom-cum-laundry.

"You're doing laundry?"

Her face clouded over. "Mom had an accident."

From her expression, it was clearly more than just wet underpants.

"Oh, that's tough," Kazumasa said. There was not much else he could say.

"I'm used to cleaning up after her—it's just that Mom gets irritable. I think she's embarrassed. Hey, hello there, Tamon."

Mayumi bent over and stretched her hand out to Tamon.

Tamon responded by sniffing her fingertips with an air of assurance, then licking them with the tip of his tongue.

"He looks smart." Mayumi patted his head.

"Told you he's a good dog."

"He seems gentle too—I'm sure Mom'll like him. Do you want to take him to see her?"

"Okay."

Kazumasa and Tamon followed Mayumi down the corridor. Their mother's room was on the ground floor at the rear. It was a sunny Japanese-style room, the biggest in the house.

"Mom, Kazumasa's here, we're coming in."

Mayumi slid open the door despite the lack of response. Inside, the air smelled of antiseptic. Kazumasa adjusted his grip on the leash and entered the room with Tamon.

"Hi, Mom. How're you feeling?"

His mother was stretched out on her side on the futon. Only her neck was bent as she stared out the window at the flower bed.

"Mom?" Kazumasa called a second time.

His mother rolled over to face him. "Who are you?"

Kazumasa bit his lip in shock. He knew his mother's symptoms were getting worse, but she had never failed to recognize him before.

"Mom, you don't know? It's Kazumasa. Your son, Kazumasa," Mayumi said with a smile. She was trying to smooth things over, but her stiff smile betrayed the shock that she, too, clearly felt.

"Oh, Kazumasa. Goodness, you have grown."

While Kazumasa stood there stunned, not knowing how to answer, Tamon walked over to his mother. He brought his nose up over her face and sniffed.

"Dear me, it's a dog . . . Is that you, Kaito?"

She stretched out her arm to stroke Tamon's chest.

"It's Kaito. Oh, I'm sure of it. Where have you been all this time?" A girlish note had entered her voice.

"Kaito?" Kazumasa said to Mayumi.

"Hmmm, I think it might be the name of her dog when she was a girl."

"Kaito, Kaito," she repeated while petting Tamon. Her mind as well as her voice seemed to have regressed to childhood.

"How long has she been this bad?" Kazumasa scrutinized his mother's face.

"The last two or three weeks. Sometimes she doesn't even know who I am."

"You should've told me . . ."

"I didn't want to worry you . . . and I knew I'd tell you eventually." Mayumi lowered her gaze.

"Ummm." Their mother sat up. "I must take Kaito for a walk."

"Good idea. Let's all go for a walk," Kazumasa promptly responded. "We can go down to the river."

THEIR MOTHER WAS IN high spirits as she walked, gripping Tamon's leash. Kazumasa was nervous about her, and from the look on Mayumi's face he guessed she felt the same. But their mother was indifferent to them. She kept up a constant stream of chatter to the dog, stopping occasionally to bend over and pet him.

"Mom looks like a girl again," Mayumi said.

"Yeah," Kazumasa agreed. It wasn't that she was looking better so much as she had become more childlike. His anxiety about her grew. There was no knowing what she might do.

Thank goodness for Tamon. It was their first outing with him in this area, but he gave the impression of being confident and in control. Kazumasa had the feeling Tamon would make sure nothing happened to his mother.

"Kazumasa, stop being such a slowpoke. Hurry up," his mother said, turning back toward him. She remembered his name now.

"You're too fast," Kazumasa said. He hurried to catch up and walk alongside her.

"Kaito's ever so smart. He stays right beside me. And he never pulls on the leash, not ever."

It wasn't only the tone of her voice but also her choice of words that made her sound childish.

"Yep. Kaito's a smart cookie all right," Kazumasa replied. He patted Tamon's head gratefully. "He's always been a smart boy, ever since he was a puppy."

Mayumi was right. Their mother was confusing Tamon with the dog she had had as a child. She was no better despite how animated she looked and sounded.

On the other side of the road, the Natori River and the fields that stretched along the river flats came into view. Kazumasa's mother stepped onto the road. There was no traffic light or pedestrian crossing.

Watch out! The words stuck in Kazumasa's throat.

Tamon stopped. Feeling the leash go tight, Kazumasa's mother stopped too.

"What is it, Kaito?" she wondered aloud, turning toward Tamon.

A truck rumbled by.

"Mom, it's dangerous to cross without looking." Mayumi's face was white.

"It's all right. Kaito's with me." She laughed innocently.

Kazumasa and Mayumi exchanged a glance. A chill, dry wind bearing hints of autumn whipped around them.

· · ·

"YOU DID GOOD TODAY, Tamon." Kazumasa stretched his arm over to the passenger seat and ruffled the fur on Tamon's chest. "You stopped Mom from running onto the road. You're like a guardian angel. Mayumi said so too."

Tamon stared straight ahead while Kazumasa stroked him.

Their walk had lasted just under an hour. Kazumasa's mother had complained of tiredness afterward and gone straight to bed. She had not left the house, let alone taken a walk, in a long time. By the time Kazumasa said goodbye, she was sleeping peacefully.

The traffic light changed. Gripping the steering wheel with both hands, Kazumasa stepped on the gas. Before the disasters he had driven a manual. Automatics weren't real cars, in his opinion. But his car had been crushed by a concrete block wall in the quake and was totaled. He didn't have the money to buy another, so Numaguchi had given him this one for work. It was a virtual wreck. Always breaking down, a gas-guzzler to boot, and it cost a heap just to keep on the road.

"Wish I could buy a real car," Kazumasa muttered.

Tamon looked at him.

"And have enough money to help Mayumi too."

Tamon faced forward again.

"I need money."

Tamon yawned.

Kazumasa parked on the shoulder near his apartment. Although it was a no-parking zone, he'd never been ticketed. Ever since the quake, the police were too busy with other stuff. Things would get back to normal one day. When that happened, he'd have to find himself a legal parking spot.

But he needed money. Really needed money.

Back inside the apartment, Kazumasa fed Tamon some dog food. His own dinner was Cup Noodles.

"You eat better than me," he said, watching Tamon wolf down his food. He yanked out a cigarette, angry at himself for even saying such a thing.

His cell phone rang. It was Mayumi.

"What's up?" he answered.

"Mom's awake, but she won't stop asking where Kaito is."

"Don't worry, I'll bring him over again."

"It's good that Tamon cheers her up, but I'm worried. She's still carrying on like a kid having a tantrum. I told her that you were the one who brought Kaito over, but she's forgotten again."

"Forgotten who I am?"

Mayumi sighed.

"We might need to put her in a home," Kazumasa said.

"Where will we get the money for that?"

There had been hardly anything left of their father's insurance payout after they paid off the mortgage on the house. Mayumi took care of their mother while living off what little remained and her own meager savings. She was able to scrape by only because of the rice and vegetables sent by their mother's relatives. Farming people.

"Really sorry, Mayumi."

"Don't be. We're family."

Kazumasa hung up and stubbed out the cigarette in the ashtray.

"Tamon, I'm gonna do it," he said. Tamon had finished his food and was lying next to Kazumasa.

"I'll take that job from Numaguchi. It's a helluva lot riskier than what I do now, but the money's good. You'll protect me, won't you? Like you protected Mom today."

Tamon's eyes were shut, but every time Kazumasa spoke, his ears gave a small twitch.

"Besides, I gotta feed you too. My mind's made up. I'll do it."

Tamon opened his eyes and looked at Kazumasa. *Why not?* those eyes seemed to say.

4

hree men emerged from the condominium block. They all had light builds and dark skin. One approached the car and knocked on the driver's window. Kazumasa lowered it.

"Kimura-san?"

This was Kazumasa's alias. "Yes."

"I'm Miguel," the man said. His Japanese was good.

"This is Jose and Ricky."

Kazumasa nodded. The names were all false anyway.

"Get in," Kazumasa said.

Miguel signaled to the other two. The man called Jose got in the front passenger seat, while Ricky and Miguel jumped in the back.

Miguel said something in a foreign language. He had noticed Tamon in the back, in the cage Kazumasa had set up for him there.

"What's a dog doing here?" Miguel asked.

"That's my *mamorigami*. Know what that is?" Kazumasa replied.

Miguel tilted his head.

"Guardian angel," Kazumasa said in English.

"Ah, I see." Miguel nodded and rattled off something to the other two.

"He won't bark or act up," Kazumasa said.

"We could do with a guardian angel. How do you say it in Japanese?"

"*Mamorigami.*"

Miguel rolled the word around in his mouth two or three times. "Okay, let's go," he said.

Kazumasa released the parking brake. Numaguchi had supplied him with a perfectly tuned Subaru Legacy for the job. Being semiautomatic, it could also be driven like a manual.

"Okay to head straight for Kokubuncho?" Kazumasa asked, giving the name of the downtown area.

Miguel nodded. It was two thirty in the morning. There was no sign of anybody around.

Kazumasa headed for the city center, taking care to avoid the N-system surveillance cameras that recorded license plates. When he started working for Numaguchi, he had researched the locations of all the N-system cameras and burned them into his memory.

"You're a good driver," said Miguel. Apparently he could tell even though they weren't going fast.

Downtown was still crowded and bright with neon lights. Kazumasa stopped the car at the corner of an office block.

"Pick us up here in thirty minutes."

Miguel and his crew got out. Tamon was lying down in his cage.

Once the three disappeared from sight, Kazumasa drove off. Despite the air conditioning, he was sweating. His throat was dry as well. He was more nervous than he realized.

He drove around aimlessly. Every time the lights of an oncoming car shined in his eyes, his heart raced. *Take it easy*, he told himself. He repeatedly checked on Tamon in the rearview mirror. Whenever he looked, Tamon was facing a different direction. Front, back, right, left. Eventually it registered: Tamon always faced south.

"What's down south?" he asked.

No reaction. Tamon stayed mute, face pointing south.

It was time. Kazumasa pulled up in the same spot where he had dropped off the men. He kept his foot over the gas pedal with the parking brake disengaged, ready to pull away instantly. His hands were sweaty on the steering wheel. He wiped his palms on his jeans, but they quickly became damp again.

"Spot anything, Tamon?" he turned to ask. Tamon looked

at him. His gaze was reassuring. *Calm down, everything will be all right*, those eyes seemed to say.

The men emerged from behind the building. Kazumasa saw that their previously empty bags were now bulging. He had been told that they planned to rob a jewelry store.

They took their time walking to the car, more like they were on their way home from a night out drinking than from a robbery.

"Come on," Kazumasa muttered under his breath. Was it his imagination, or did he hear alarms and the blare of police sirens? He pictured the police in pursuit of him. The image played over and over in his mind. He could push the Subaru to its limits all he liked, but in the end he would still get caught.

"Let's go," Miguel said as he got in the front passenger seat. Jose and Ricky climbed into the back.

They shut the doors, and Kazumasa gunned the accelerator.

"Easy now. No need to hurry. Take it slow, okay?" Miguel lightly tapped Kazumasa's left hand on the steering wheel."

"Sorry."

Kazumasa eased his foot off the pedal slightly. If he drew attention to them now, it would only defeat the purpose. He needed to drive slowly to stay off the police's radar.

"That's some guardian angel you've got." Miguel turned to look in the rear. Tamon was facing south again.

Kazumasa licked his lips. Stay calm, he told himself as he drove, making sure to avoid the N-system cameras.

The men laughed, smoked, and talked among themselves in a language Kazumasa did not understand. They were so relaxed that Kazumasa never would have guessed they were fresh from committing a crime. He took a circuitous route back to the condo where he had picked them up.

"Thanks, Kimura-san. See you again," Miguel said with a smile as he got out.

The other two followed him. They left without looking back.

Kazumasa called Numaguchi on his smartphone. "Just finished."

"Whoa. Good work. Go home and rest."

"Will do."

"Check your mailbox."

"Mailbox? Why?"

The line cut off before Kazumasa finished speaking. He clicked his tongue in annoyance and drove off.

"Sorry about the bad company, Tamon. Let's go home and hit the sack."

Tamon had turned again to face south.

Back at his apartment, Kazumasa checked his mailbox. He found a brown envelope. He grabbed it and hurried inside, then locked the door firmly behind him. As he wiped Tamon's feet clean by the door, he concentrated on getting his breathing under control.

First he gave Tamon some water. Then he sat down on the tatami and smoked a cigarette before picking up the envelope. Inside were twenty 10,000-yen bills. In one night he had made as much as he usually earned in a month. *Far out. If only I could do a job like this once a week.*

"I could make things easier for Mayumi," Kazumasa mumbled, lighting another cigarette.

Tamon came over to his side and lay down. He shut his eyes and immediately started snoring.

"Tired, buddy?" Kazumasa asked softly. He counted the 10,000-yen bills again.

5

very channel carried the same story. Three thieves were on the run after a jewelry store heist in Kokuncho in the early hours of the morning. The haul was one million yen worth of jewelry and luxury watches.

Security cameras captured the whole thing. The men wore ski masks and used a crowbar to smash a window. Once inside, they broke open the display case and filled their bags with jewelry and watches. The entire process took roughly five minutes from start to finish.

The TV announcer said that police were treating it as the work of an organized crime gang, based on how smooth an operation it was.

"Holy shit." Kazumasa shook when he saw the footage. Until now he hadn't felt like part of the robbery. He had been merely the driver. But seeing the video of the actual crime made him realize he was an accomplice.

The twenty 10,000-yen bills were no longer any comfort. If

Mayumi found out where the money came from, she would flip out.

"But money is money," he murmured, trying to convince himself.

And he needed money to survive. Besides, he had a mother with dementia who was rapidly declining. And a sister sacrificing herself for their mother.

HE NEEDED MONEY. And he would take any kind of job to get it. The earthquake, tsunami, and nuclear disasters earlier that year had wiped out lots of jobs. Kazumasa was ready to clutch at any straw. And right then that straw happened to be Miguel and his men. It was criminal, he knew, but if that was the only thing going, then he would take it. If he didn't, Mayumi and his mother would not survive.

"Tamon, walk time," he said to the sleeping dog. Tamon jumped to his feet and headed for the door. The way he moved, it was like he'd been living in the apartment for years.

Most of the other residents in the apartment building were single. They all had daytime jobs and had already left for work, so there was nobody around to ask Kazumasa what a dog was doing there.

Kazumasa set off for a walk with Tamon, going nowhere in

particular. He had looked up online how to care for a dog. One article said that dogs should be walked at least twice a day for more than thirty minutes each time.

Tamon kept pace with Kazumasa, never straining on the leash. He always stayed on Kazumasa's left. He stopped to urinate on utility poles and signs, but that was all.

"Your owner sure did a good job training you."

Kazumasa was impressed. The only dogs he'd known were small ones that yanked on their leash, went wherever they wanted, and yapped hysterically at every other dog or person they encountered. Tamon was clearly not that kind of dog. He walked with assurance, putting his trust in the human who held the leash, but not one hundred percent. He was the perfect partner.

Kazumasa went to turn left down a side street and almost knocked into Tamon. Tamon was trying to go right.

"Huh? You want to go that way?"

Kazumasa wasn't heading anywhere special, so he decided to follow Tamon's lead.

At the next side street Kazumasa tried to turn right, but Tamon resisted. He wanted to go straight ahead.

"We can't go straight. It leads to the main road. It'll be hard to walk there with all the people and cars," Kazumasa said.

Tamon came to a halt, still facing straight ahead.

"Come on, buddy, this way."

Kazumasa tugged on the leash, but then it dawned on him: Tamon was trying to go south.

"Hey, what's down south? Your owner? Or maybe that's where you used to live?"

Tamon looked at Kazumasa.

"If I knew where you wanted to go, I'd take you there. But I don't, so I can't help. Sorry, buddy."

Kazumasa pulled lightly on the leash. This time Tamon obeyed him instantly. They turned right down a side street and continued walking.

So, Tamon wanted to go south. Kazumasa was sure of it.

KAZUMASA WAS RINSING OUT Tamon's bowl when Numaguchi called.

"See the news?"

"Yeah."

"Those guys are hot shit. Gotta hand it to them."

"Who are they?"

"Dunno much. They started in Tokyo, then Osaka, and now they're going around Japan. I got asked to look after them in Sendai, in return for a percentage of their loot."

"I see."

The last haul had been around 100 million yen. A small percentage of that would be several million yen. Numaguchi was still making a nice profit after paying Kazumasa his 200,000 yen.

"So, they're on again next week."

"Next week? For real? The cops'll still be sniffing around."

"That's their MO. Move in, make a killing in a short time, then move on."

Kazumasa stifled a sigh. There went his hope of regularly making 200,000 yen. Miguel and his gang were not going to hang around Sendai long.

"The one called Miguel says he likes your guardian angel. What's he mean, guardian angel?"

"The dog."

"*That* dog? Strange. Anyway, I'll be in touch with details."

"Gotcha. I'll be waiting."

Kazumasa hung up.

"I knew it was too good to last," he said to Tamon.

Tamon turned to face Kazumasa. *That's how it goes*, he seemed to say.

KAZUMASA'S MOTHER MAY HAVE forgotten who her son was, but she certainly didn't forget Tamon.

She beckoned him into the room with a broad smile and patted him on the head, cooing, "Kaito, Kaito." Tamon didn't seem to object.

"Mayumi, got a minute?" Kazumasa called his sister into the kitchen.

"What's up?"

"This. It's not a lot, but put it toward something."

He handed Mayumi the brown envelope. There was 100,000 yen inside.

Mayumi opened the envelope, then gave him a puzzled look.

"Where'd this come from?"

"Just a bit of extra income. I won at pachinko two days in a row." Kazumasa gave the spiel he'd prepared.

"You've been gambling?" she demanded.

"Pachinko doesn't count as gambling. I was just killing time and ended up winning."

"Don't get too excited and make a habit of it."

"I won't."

"Anyway, thanks for this. It helps." Mayumi pressed the envelope to her chest and nodded in gratitude.

"Quit that. We're family."

"But you have to be thankful for things. Work going okay?"

"Yeah. I'm used to it now. I should get paid soon. For what it's worth."

Kazumasa had given Mayumi a story about working as a driver for a delivery service. Mayumi knew Numaguchi. If she realized Kazumasa was working for him, it would only cause her grief. Her hands were full enough looking after their mother. Kazumasa didn't want to give her anything else to worry about.

"Don't waste it all; put some into savings. When Mom gets worse I won't be able to care for her all by myself. We'll need the money."

"How much of Dad's insurance is left?"

"About three million, I think."

"Is that all . . . ? I should find work in Tokyo."

"I might need you to think seriously about that," Mayumi replied gravely.

They could hear laughter coming from their mother's room. Under normal circumstances it would have been a welcome sound, but given their mother's condition, it only wrung their hearts.

"Let's go for a walk with Tamon," Kazumasa said. "All of us."

Mayumi nodded. "Mom likes going for a walk when Tamon's here. Otherwise she'd spend all day inside."

She stuffed the envelope of cash in the back pocket of her jeans and removed her apron. "Mom, do you want to go for a walk with Tamon?"

"Yes, oh, yes."

The girlish voice was no surprise.

THEY TOOK A DIFFERENT route this time, cutting along a path beside the vegetable fields to get to the Natori River. They drew closer to the riverbank and came upon a small park with a row of benches.

The three of them sat on one bench, and Kazumasa put the bag dangling from his right hand beside him. Along the way they had stopped at a convenience store to buy sandwiches, rice balls, and drinks.

"Great weather, isn't it?" Mayumi looked up at the sky. It was a cloudless day, neither too hot nor too cold. The breeze blowing off the river felt pleasant after working up a sweat on their walk.

"Mom, do you want something to eat?" Kazumasa asked.

"Ham sandwich," she promptly replied.

Kazumasa smiled as he removed the wrapping from the ham sandwich. He poked a straw in a paper carton of orange juice and handed the juice to his mother.

"Can I give Kaito some?" she asked Mayumi, taking the sandwich.

"No, you can't. Human food is poison to dogs."

Their mother's face clouded over.

Kazumasa took a packet of chicken jerky from the bag. "Here, Mom, give him this."

"Really?" She took the bag of jerky. Tamon's ears pricked up. No doubt he remembered the jerky that Kazumasa had given him when they first met.

Their mother fed it to Tamon. Tamon wagged his tail vigorously and chewed.

"Good boy, Kaito." She smiled in delight and stared at Tamon.

"You eat something, too, Mom," Mayumi said.

Her mother took a bite of the sandwich.

"We'll eat too. I'm hungry," Mayumi said. She had a potato salad sandwich and Kazumasa a cod roe rice ball. They drank bottles of iced oolong tea.

After lunch, Kazumasa stood up and walked off a little way to have a smoke.

His mother kept up her chatter with Tamon while Mayumi watched over them with a smile. They were, to all appearances, a perfect family. Tamon's presence and the mild early autumn sunshine only added to the idyllic picture.

Kazumasa finished his cigarette and returned to the bench. He noticed tears in Mayumi's eyes.

"What's wrong, Mayumi?"

"I was just thinking how happy I am. It's been tough. But then I come down to the river on a beautiful day like this, have a picnic, hear Mom laugh, and somehow it made me think that maybe this is what heaven is like. Then the tears just came."

Kazumasa put his arm around her shoulder.

"It's hard to believe that six months ago we were in a living hell," she said.

"It's thanks to Tamon," said Kazumasa.

"Sure is. Thanks to him, Mom's got some life back, and we can all go out for a walk as a family. It really is thanks to Tamon."

Tamon's eyes were pinned on their mother. Perhaps he knew there was still some jerky left. But she took it as a sign of his affection and was over the moon.

How long had it been since they'd seen Mom smile? Mayumi was right: This might be what heaven was. Warm, peaceful, and happy.

Tamon had brought Kazumasa and his family closer to heaven.

6

Miguel and his crew got in the car. As before, Jose sat in the front. Miguel twisted around in the back seat to poke his finger through the cage and stroke Tamon under the chin.

"All will go well again today with our guardian angel here," Miguel said.

"I see you like Tamon," said Kazumasa, stepping on the gas.

"What does the name Tamon mean?"

"Beats me." Kazumasa shrugged. "He's a stray. His collar had Tamon written on it. So I thought it was his name."

"A stray . . . After the tsunami?"

"Prob'ly. The owner either died or was separated from Tamon."

Once again Miguel turned around to speak to Tamon. Kazumasa had no idea what language he spoke but guessed he said something along the lines of *you poor dog*.

Miguel liked dogs, it seemed.

Kazumasa had been instructed by Numaguchi to take the

gang to the Nagamachi-Minami station on the Namboku subway line. He dropped them near the subway entrance.

"Meet back here in thirty minutes," Miguel said before disappearing into the night.

Again Kazumasa drove about aimlessly. And again he returned to the same spot thirty minutes later. The three men soon appeared. As before, they were cool and collected.

Kazumasa was less nervous this time. He drove off, not speaking unnecessarily and avoiding the N-system cameras. People could get used to anything. In the distance he heard the scream of police sirens, but they were not headed in their direction. Miguel and his gang were pros. No doubt they scoped out their targets with great care before carrying out their raids. Knowing the layout of everything in advance was part of the job. They were experts at robbing jewelry stores, then escaping before the police arrived.

As before, Kazumasa dropped the men a short distance from the condo. Jose and Ricky jumped out quickly and took off. Miguel remained in the car.

"What is it?" Kazumasa asked. He was on edge.

"Will you give me your guardian angel?" Miguel said.

"Tamon? No way. He's my dog."

"How about for five hundred thousand yen?"

Kazumasa had been about to tell Miguel to hurry up and get out but swallowed his words instead. "Five hundred thou?"

"Give me the dog and I'll pay it."

"Why so much?"

"He's a great dog. A guardian angel. He will bring me good luck. With him around, the cops will never catch get me. Is five hundred thousand not enough? How about a million?"

Kazumasa wavered. It would take him months to earn that much, and now he had the chance to make it on the spot. All he had to do was hand over Tamon. Sure, he liked Tamon, but he'd taken him in only recently. One million yen was a lot of money. With that much, he could really help Mayumi.

The thought of Mayumi's and his mother's happiness was almost enough to make him do it. Especially since Miguel liked dogs. Miguel was sure to treat Tamon well and take good care of him. Then Kazumasa's eyes met Tamon's. Those eyes bored into his skull, as if he could read Kazumasa's mind.

"Can't do it." Kazumasa shook his head. "Tamon's family. I wouldn't sell him at any price."

"I see. I'm sorry, but I understand how you feel. A dog is precious. You're right."

Miguel got out of the car. He said something to Tamon that Kazumasa didn't understand.

"I'll see you again. Make sure to bring the guardian angel."

Kazumasa nodded. Miguel turned his back and walked away.

"Sorry, Tamon, for a moment there I almost did something

stupid. After what you've done for us . . . the happiness you've brought my family."

Kazumasa drove west to an interchange on the Tohoku Expressway. His apartment was in the opposite direction, but Kazumasa didn't feel like sleeping just yet. He wanted to go for a drive. Fast. He hadn't done that in a long while.

He looked in the rearview mirror, and it was no surprise to see Tamon facing south.

AFTER EXITING THE EXPRESSWAY at the Sendai-Tobu Airport Interchange, Kazumasa headed toward the ocean. He'd been avoiding the coast ever since the tsunami. The landscape still bore fresh scars of the destruction. And he was still afraid. But six months had passed, and he had a new family member—a dog called Tamon. It was time to pull himself together and put things behind him. Despite everything, he felt like seeing the ocean.

There was no sign of the homes and warehouses that used to dot the area before the tsunami. And the windbreak pine forest that once lined the coast was gone, swallowed by the waves.

Kazumasa stopped the car. He let Tamon out and headed toward the sea. It was nearly dawn. The horizon was turning red, little by little. A sea breeze that would have been pleasant during the day felt cold on his skin.

A sign of how quickly autumn had advanced. Stars twin-
kled in a moonless sky. He heard the lonely sound of waves
lapping on the sand.

Kazumasa walked in silence along the shore. First he went
north. Tamon followed directly behind. After a while he rotated and turned right. Tamon immediately sped up. For some
reason, Tamon was drawn to the south.

Kazumasa removed the leash. Tamon stopped and turned
to look behind him.

"Off you go, buddy," Kazumasa said. "You wanna go south,
right? Somebody waiting for you there? Someone special? It's
okay. Get going. Go where you want."

Kazumasa himself didn't know why he came out with this.
Tamon meant a lot to him. If Tamon disappeared from his life,
of course he would miss him, and so would his mother. Her
symptoms might even get worse.

Yet still he listened to the whisper deep in his heart, that he
should set Tamon free to go where he wanted.

"Off you go," Kazumasa said. Tamon looked at him, then
turned to face south. He narrowed his eyes and sniffed the air.
His legs were tensed and ready, as if preparing to race off at
any moment.

Although Kazumasa had told Tamon to go, the thought of
him actually leaving broke his heart.

But Tamon had his own family. They just happened to be

separated from each other right now. Somehow, Kazumasa understood that Tamon was on a journey in search of his family and that he was no more than a temporary companion whom Tamon had met along the way. Having that knowledge, he didn't feel he could hold Tamon back. It would be a betrayal of the affection Tamon had shown him.

The tension drained from Tamon's body. He stopped sniffing the air and walked over to Kazumasa. Then he pressed himself against Kazumasa's thigh, as if asking to be petted.

"Sure you don't wanna go?" asked Kazumasa.

Tamon wagged his tail.

"Really sure? Aren't you desperate to find somebody?"

Tamon remained pressed against Kazumasa's thigh, making no move to leave.

"Thanks," said Kazumasa.

The word came from his heart. He'd never been more grateful to anyone in his life.

"Thank you, Tamon."

He squatted down to hug Tamon. Tamon pressed his nose against Kazumasa's cheek. His nose was ice-cold.

7

"P achinko, again?" Mayumi looked suspiciously at the money Kazumasa had given her.

"Yeah. Beginner's luck, I guess."

"Didn't I tell you not to gamble?"

"I won't anymore. My luck'll run out soon."

Kazumasa and Mayumi left the store and headed for the car. They were on their way to Mount Zao after Kazumasa had suggested going for a long drive. Along the way their mother had complained of hunger, so they were stopped at a bakery to buy sweet buns and sandwiches.

"You bring Tamon around almost every day, and you're driving a new car—what's going on? You can't be working."

The look Mayumi gave him stabbed Kazumasa in the heart.

"I'm winning at pachinko, so I took a break from work." He wanted it to sound like a joke, but Mayumi didn't soften her expression.

"You're not involved in anything sus, are you?"

"What do you mean, 'sus'?"

"I heard a rumor you're working for Numaguchi. Is it true?"

"That goon Numaguchi? Don't make me laugh." Kazumasa denied it with a straight face. Mayumi's instincts had always been unerring.

"Kazumasa." She grabbed his hand, and he stopped in his tracks. He knew from the way she said his name that he was in for it.

"You're all I've got. Get it? If you don't get your shit together, what will become of Mom and me?"

"I know, I know." Kazumasa sulked.

"There's no such thing as easy money. You could do any number of things. With all the rebuilding after the earthquake and the tsunami—there's a shortage of labor."

"I told you, I know. Don't get so uptight—you'll ruin the day."

Kazumasa brushed off Mayumi's hand and walked away. Their mother was laughing in the back seat of the car and talking to Tamon through the mesh of his cage.

Kazumasa's sister's words stung. But Kazumasa didn't want to argue and risk removing the smile from his mother's face.

"I'll get a proper job," he turned to say to Mayumi as he was getting back in the car.

Miguel and his men would soon leave Sendai. It would mean the end of his easy money. Kazumasa would have to find a job. Up till now he'd shied away from manual labor, but he couldn't make any more excuses. He couldn't let things with Numaguchi drag on any longer.

"I got you a ham sandwich." Kazumasa handed his mother a bag with her favorite sandwich in it.

"Thank you, Kazu-chan," she said.

He was touched. She hadn't called him that since junior high school. Her memory might be shot, but his mother still recognized him.

"Kaito says he wants to go for a walk."

"Won't be long till we're at a big park. We'll walk him there."

"Okay."

Mayumi got in the front seat. Kazumasa started the engine.

"I love Kaito," their mother said, and took a bite of her ham sandwich.

"We all love Kaito, don't we?" Kazumasa said as he backed the car out.

"Kaito says he loves us too," his mother said.

The look on her face was one of pure happiness.

TEN DAYS AFTER THE second heist, Numaguchi contacted Kazumasa again. Rendezvous with the gang, drop them at the designated place, meet up and take them back to the condo. It was easy work. There was little worry of being chased by cops, either. Miguel and his men were pros.

"I guess that's the last job for this lot in Sendai," said Numaguchi. "How about some more work in the same line after they go?"

"No more. Please. My family is worried about me. Once this is over, I'm looking for a proper job."

"Okay, then. Not forcing you. Just take care of this last one." Numaguchi laughed and hung up.

Kazumasa had given half his earnings so far to Mayumi and kept the rest, but he hadn't touched it yet. This job would net him another 200,000 yen. With 400,000 yen cash in hand, he could survive while he looked for proper work.

"Let's go," Kazumasa said to Tamon. Tamon was lying next to the door. He stood at the sound of Kazumasa's voice and stretched. He had picked up the signals from Kazumasa's body language and seemed to understand that they were going out tonight. Tamon was a master at mind reading.

When Kazumasa opened the back of the car, Tamon leapt into the luggage section. He entered the cage freely and waited for Kazumasa to shut the door.

"This is the last time, buddy. Your job's to protect us." Kazumasa put his hands together in a gesture of prayer.

Tamon yawned.

It was nearly October, and a chill was setting in. Kazumasa's breath turned white.

Kazumasa sat in the driver's seat, started up the car, and lit a cigarette. Then he opened a window so Tamon wouldn't breathe the smoke. Instantly the temperature inside the car plunged. It was unbearable. Kazumasa stubbed out his cigarette and raised the window.

"I never cared about anyone's health when I had a smoke before," he said to Tamon.

Tamon's face was pointing south.

The gang were waiting in the usual place. Tonight, too, Miguel sat in the back. He said something to Tamon and smiled. Then he said, "Kokubuncho."

"Again?"

The first job had been in Kokubuncho. Kazumasa thought they must be out of their minds to try a second time in the same area.

"The cops' guard'll be down. They won't be expecting us in the same place again."

Kazumasa nodded and drove in the direction of Kokubuncho. They were the experts. It wasn't for an amateur like himself to butt in.

"Tonight's our last job in Sendai," Miguel announced. "So I will ask again: Can I have your guardian angel?"

Kazumasa shook his head. "No can do."

"I see." Miguel laughed and did not press the issue.

Kazumasa dropped the men to the outskirts of Kokubuncho and drove around to kill time. As Miguel predicted, Kazumasa didn't see a single patrol car or police officer in the vicinity. Nearly three weeks had passed since the first heist. Maybe the investigation in this area was finished.

Kazumasa returned to the same spot thirty minutes later. Miguel and his men got in. They were cool and collected. Not a bead of sweat on them.

"Kimura-san, thanks for taking care of us. Sendai's a great city. I want to come back."

"Where are you going next?"

In the rearview mirror Kazumasa could see Miguel smile wryly.

"That's a secret."

"Oh, of course. Stupid question." He shut his mouth and concentrated on driving.

The three were more talkative than usual. Kazumasa guessed they were more relaxed because it was their last job in Sendai.

The condo block came into view. Kazumasa eased his foot off the gas pedal.

He saw Tamon in the rearview mirror. "Huh?" There was something different about him. Kazumasa strained to look more carefully. Tamon was pointing in the direction of the condo. Why would he face that way instead of his usual south?

Kazumasa's doubts grew as he stepped on the brake. Tamon began growling just before the car came to a complete halt.

"What's up, Tamon?" He pulled on the parking brake and turned to look in the back. Tamon had never behaved like this before.

Suddenly, Miguel let out a yell. Jose and Ricky scrambled to get out of the car. Less than two car lengths ahead, three men stood in the road swinging metal bats and iron pipes. They had burst out from a side street. Another three emerged behind the car from a different side street.

"Drive!" Miguel screamed.

Kazumasa released the parking brake and shifted into drive. Jose had gotten back in the car, but Ricky was still struggling to get in on the front passenger side. He had one leg in and one out.

"Hurry!" Miguel shouted.

"But Ricky—"

"If you don't want to die, drive now!"

Reflexively, Kazumasa stepped on the pedal. Ricky tumbled onto the sidewalk. The men on the street raised a ruckus.

"Hit the gas!" Miguel yelled.

"Yeah, yeah."

One man stood in their way, legs planted akimbo in the middle of the street. Kazumasa turned the steering wheel hard to one side. The car skidded, and the tires squealed. Kazumasa just managed to avoid hitting the man. A wall loomed ahead. Then a HiAce van came barreling out of a side street. Kazumasa slammed on the brakes. The wall was just feet away. They were going to hit it.

Kazumasa banged his head. He heard Tamon bark, then a tremendous crashing sound, and then darkness swallowed him.

KAZUMASA AWOKE IN AGONY and groaned. His head hurt, his throat hurt, his sides hurt. The car was filled with smoke. Kazumasa's body was trembling.

Gradually, he remembered: the van had smashed into them from the side.

"Tamon," he called, but there was no response.

Grimacing with pain, Kazumasa unbuckled his seat belt and tried to get out. The door was buckled. It wouldn't budge.

"Please. I don't care about myself; I gotta help Tamon."

Kazumasa rammed the door with his shoulder, and it swung open. He fell out. He tried to stand and discovered that his lower body could not support him. Sweat trickled into his eyes. He wiped his forehead and flinched when his fingers came in contact with something that did not feel like sweat. His forehead was covered in blood.

It was cold. Freezing cold. Kazumasa shivered. His teeth chattered.

He could hear groaning and rolled his body over on the asphalt to look for the source of the voices. He saw bodies writhing on the road, just as he was. The same men who had sprung at them from a side street. Their metal bats and iron pipes lay scattered on the ground.

Where was Tamon? Where was Miguel?

Kazumasa craned his neck to look around. He found Miguel. But not Jose or Ricky. Miguel was visible in the light from a streetlamp. He was covered in blood. In his right hand he held a knife, and in his left, a piece of string.

String? No, a leash, not string. Tamon's leash.

Kazumasa followed it with his eyes. He saw Tamon walking behind Miguel.

"Tamon!" he cried. But what was meant as a yell came out weakly.

Tamon stopped just the same and turned around to look.

"Tamon . . . Tamon."

Tamon tried to approach him. But the instant he reached the end of his leash, he was dragged back by Miguel.

"Wait for me, Tamon—"

Kazumasa stretched out his arm. But Miguel leaned over and picked up Tamon, then fled with the dog in his arms.

"Tamon . . ." Kazumasa could not stop shaking. The pain was getting worse.

Where are you taking Tamon, Miguel? What will happen to my mother and sister?

Tamon and Miguel disappeared from sight.

"Sorry, Mom. Sorry, Mayumi," Kazumasa mumbled, then closed his eyes.

ii

The Thief
and the Dog

The Thief

1

Miguel snapped the knife blade shut and slid it into his back pocket. He felt a tug on the leash. The dog was looking around for its owner. He reprimanded it sharply. Too bad, but that'd been a massive crash. The Japanese guy was a goner.

Miguel could still hear angry shouting. The yakuza were after him.

"Let's go," he said to the dog, pulling lightly on the leash to urge him along.

They fled down one narrow street after another. Making their way through the dark, away from the glare of the streetlamps. Miguel didn't know the area well, but he could find his way on dark roads easily enough. Darkness had been Miguel's home ever since he could remember.

After a while, the dog stopped looking back. Smart dog. He'd accepted Miguel as his new boss. It wasn't that the dog didn't care about the Japanese guy. He'd simply switched gears in order to survive.

"Good boy." Miguel stroked the dog's head. He was his guardian angel. As long as he had the dog with him, he would be safe from bad luck.

"Tamon?" Miguel said, trying out the name the Japanese guy had used.

The dog, Tamon, looked up.

"Tamon, from now on you belong to me," Miguel informed him.

THE CAR WAS STILL in the coin parking lot where he'd left it the day before. Miguel had prepared himself an escape vehicle in case the need arose. Takahashi didn't know about it.

He had gotten himself a secondhand Volkswagen SUV. Miguel loaded Tamon into the cargo space, paid the parking fee, and started the engine. They drove away quietly.

Tamon seemed relaxed. This dog was not only smart, he also had nerves of steel. In the wild he'd have been the leader of the pack. He had that quality.

Miguel headed south, weaving his way through the back streets. Every time he entered a new district, he checked for N-system and other security surveillance cameras. He couldn't afford to be spotted by the police.

Once he was out of the Sendai city limits and in the neighboring city of Natori, he drove along the national route. Keeping strictly to the speed limit, he regularly checked the rearview mirror for tails. He saw nothing.

He was working on the assumption that Jose and Ricky had been caught. If they'd survived, they were being tortured, but they wouldn't be able to say in which direction Miguel was fleeing, because they didn't know.

"Sorry, partners."

Miguel put a cigarette in his mouth and lit it. He opened the window wide, careful not to let smoke drift back to the cargo space. Smoking was a bad habit of humans. He didn't want to inflict it on the dog.

"Do you miss the Japanese guy?" Miguel asked Tamon in his mother tongue.

Tamon stared straight ahead. Come to think of it, Tamon always had his nose pointed south whenever they were out on a job.

So Tamon wanted to go south. "Didn't you belong to him? You got family down south?"

Tamon gave no answer.

MIGUEL STOPPED THE VOLKSWAGEN at a convenience store where there was a row of trucks lined up in the parking lot.

He went inside to pick up sweet buns, a drink, and food for the dog. Tossing his purchases on the back seat, he walked over to the ashtray stand, lit a cigarette, and made a phone call.

"Takahashi double-crossed me. Jose and Ricky are either dead or caught," he said in English when the phone on the other end picked up.

"How much did you make there?"

"Just a cut on what we stole."

"I bet they didn't want to give that up. Rumor is Takahashi and his gang have money troubles."

Miguel made a sound of disgust. He'd guessed that was the reason for what happened. But it was still a dirty trick.

"I wanna get out of the country. Help me."

"S'not easy. First get yourself to Korea or Russia. Then I can help."

"I don't need help once I'm outta here."

"I know, but I can't do anything to get you out of Japan."

"Got it. I'll be in touch."

Miguel hung up. He stuck another cigarette in his mouth and lit it. While blowing out plumes of smoke, he conjured up a map of Japan in his head and searched his memory for what others in his line of work had said. Niigata was the best prefecture to exit the country. From there it was easy to access Russia and the Korean Peninsula.

"Niigata . . ." He put out his cigarette, returned to the car, and got in the back seat. Tamon poked his nose over the backrest.

"Hungry?" Miguel said in his own language.

Tamon wrinkled his nose. Miguel opened the packet of dog food, transferred it to a paper bowl, and placed it on the floor in the back.

Tamon began eating. The slightly raised fur on the dog's back told Miguel that Tamon was still vigilant even while wolfing down food. This dog might be on the road with Miguel, because that was how things had turned out, but he wasn't forming a new pack anytime soon.

"You're one smart, brave dog," he muttered. "You have a big heart."

Miguel desperately wanted for Tamon to be his dog. Somehow he had to win him over. He was planning on taking Tamon home with him. Which meant leaving the country by ship, not plane.

"Niigata . . ."

He got in the driver's seat and started the engine.

2

The beach was visible from where Miguel parked the car. Tsunami debris still littered the coastal area. Six months after the massive quake, recovery in Minamisoma had barely begun.

Miguel let Tamon out and attached the leash, then started trudging along the coastline. Tamon walked alongside, matching his pace to Miguel's, never pulling on the leash.

"Good boy," Miguel said in English.

Tamon gave no reaction.

"So who's down south?"

He knew it was pointless asking but couldn't help himself. Tamon lifted a leg in reply and peed on a clump of grass.

"As you like. Just wait, you won't be able to ignore me for long."

They saw no one. The tsunami was still fresh in people's memories, making them wary of going near the sea. A normal enough reaction.

After ten minutes or so, Miguel saw a building he remembered. Before the tsunami, it had been a seafood-processing plant. Though damaged, the concrete walls and roof were still in place. The company that owned it had gone out of business, and nobody went there anymore.

Miguel entered the building with Tamon. It was dark, and he stopped and closed his eyes for a few seconds. Upon opening them again, things started to come into focus.

To the rear of the building was a barricade made of broken machinery and piles of rubble. Miguel knew that a door on the other side led to another room. Probably what used to be the staff changing room.

He hooked Tamon's leash on the leg of an upturned desk, then began tearing down the barricade. It was hard work on his own, taking apart what had taken three of them to build. He slogged on in silence.

After half an hour, the door showed through the rubble. Though warped and battered by the tsunami, it still held fast. When Miguel turned the doorknob and leaned his weight against the door, it creaked open.

The room was exactly as he'd last seen it a month earlier. A row of lockers, the leftmost one still with a brand-new combination lock. Miguel rotated the dial and unlocked it.

Inside the locker was a small suitcase. He checked the contents. It was stuffed with 10,000-yen bills—the gang's payment for their work in Japan. Enough for Miguel to spend the rest of his life back home on easy street. If he was on his own, that was—he would need at least three times that amount to support a family. Ten times more if he split it evenly with Jose and Ricky.

He and Jose and Ricky had been lured to Fukushima Prefecture with the promise of making that money. Takahashi had invited them. They had been tempted by the fact that stealing would be a breeze in the immediate aftermath of the disasters. And it was true that working here was easier than working in Tokyo or Osaka. But Miguel felt sick about it. He'd seen people here who had lost homes and family, and in them he saw himself as a boy.

Miguel had grown up dirt poor. He had been born and raised in a garbage dump. Where his family lived could hardly be called a house. Its roof was made from cardboard boxes and sheets of galvanized iron. For as long as he could remember, Miguel had scavenged the mountain of trash for things to sell. That was how his family lived. They were destitute, life was hard, and his family was his sole pillar of support.

Many people in the disaster zone had lost loved ones in the tsunami and no longer had even family to lean on. Working in the area made Miguel feel he may as well have been stealing directly from disaster victims.

With every job, Miguel told himself he was doing it for the

money, to make things easier for his family. The reward for all his work was in this suitcase.

"Let's go."

Miguel unhooked Tamon's leash. He picked up the suitcase in his right hand and held the leash in his left.

"I have to split the money with Ricky's and Jose's families."

Tamon's ears pricked up when Miguel started speaking.

"It's only right. I'll use the rest to start some kind of business. Make things easier for my sister. I'll buy her a house too. I've had enough of being a thief."

Tamon looked behind him. The car was in the direction opposite to the one Tamon wanted to go in.

"Keep walking straight. Once we're in the car we'll go south again."

Miguel was lying. To get to Niigata they had to go west.

Takahashi and the others would be hell-bent on coming after him—or rather, coming after the money. Miguel planned to take his time getting to Niigata, using regular roads and avoiding the expressway.

Once they reached the car, Miguel made Tamon get in the cargo space again. Tamon immediately crouched down, and Miguel stroked his back. The soft fur felt good.

"Where I come from might be too hot for you. Don't worry. I'll keep the air conditioning on high."

He placed the suitcase in the back seat. Then he removed several bills from it and put them in his wallet.

"I could use some food," Miguel mumbled, and put a cigarette in his mouth.

MIGUEL DECIDED TO SPEND the night in the parking lot of a shopping mall on the outskirts of Koriyama city. His stomach protested noisily at an evening meal that consisted of only sweet bread and canned coffee, but Miguel ignored it. An empty stomach was Miguel's friend. His constant companion ever since he was small.

Miguel crawled into the back of the car with Tamon and lay on his side, knees up. He didn't need a mattress or futon. Anywhere was a thousand times better than sleeping on a pile of garbage.

Tamon lay facedown. Miguel put his hand on the dog's back, but Tamon didn't stir an inch. He knew Miguel was not hostile.

"You searching for a friend?" Miguel asked.

Tamon gave no reaction.

"Have you ever heard a foreign language? Do I have to speak Japanese?"

Tamon closed his eyes. *I can't keep up with all your talk*, it seemed to Miguel he was saying.

"You are one proud dog." Miguel smiled. "My first friend was a dog. A stray. A dirty, skinny thing, but proud, like you," he said.

Tamon snored.

Many other families besides Miguel's lived in the garbage dump. They were all equally poor. Their houses had roofs but no walls, and they made a living by scavenging. They were comrades and rivals. Each fought to gain an advantage in searching the garbage for treasure. That was what they had to do to survive.

Miguel was the youngest of the gang of kids who lived there. Only babies and toddlers were younger. Most of the time the older boys and girls were playmates, but when it came to work, they were rivals, as fierce and relentless as vultures.

Whenever Miguel found something of value, by some sixth sense the others would appear from nowhere and swoop down to snatch his find from him. He put up a good fight but could never match the big kids in strength and inevitably went to bed crying. If he complained to his parents or sister, they only scolded him for not making it home with his finds before the others caught up with him.

Eventually, Miguel stopped speaking. He left the gang of kids who hung out together and went off on his own, scavenging in silence. The others started treating him as a rebel for deserting them, and their attacks became even more merciless. He was beaten, cursed, and spat upon.

One day, Miguel found a pocketknife. The handle was decrepit and the blade so red with rust he couldn't even open it. But with a rag and scraps of worn-out sandpaper he found in the garbage, he persisted with cleaning it until all the rust was gone. After a month the knife was gleaming. He sharpened the blade with a stone and wound a rag around the handle. Then he wrapped the knife in newspaper and kept it in his pocket.

A few days later, when he was scavenging through the garbage, Miguel deliberately cried out, as if he'd found something. The vultures swarmed and demanded he hand it over. Miguel pulled the knife from his pocket and slashed at the nearest boy. Blood spurted, and the boy screamed.

Miguel continued to swing the knife wildly until someone grabbed his arm. Then he found himself knocked off his feet and onto the garbage, the knife ripped from his hand, and pummeled by countless fists and feet. By the time Miguel's parents arrived, his whole body was swollen, bruised, and covered in blood.

He couldn't get up for a week. When he was able to stand again and go back to work, the other kids didn't take his finds anymore. Instead, they ignored him. Nobody would speak to him or meet his eyes. They treated him as if he didn't exist, and if he ever came near anybody, they moved away, as if by an unspoken understanding.

Miguel was a ghost. A child ghost. Wandering the mountain of trash. Day after day he rooted through the garbage by himself, never even turning his head toward the voices of the other children at play. He simply kept working.

One day he was going to leave all this. He would live in a proper house and always have enough to eat. This was all he could think about.

Then came a day when it had been raining since morning. Miguel was searching through the garbage as usual and getting soaked to the bone. All of a sudden he sensed a presence behind him and quickly turned around. Nobody except for his family had come this close to him since the knife incident.

Miguel saw a dog staring at him.

A short-haired mongrel. Like Miguel, it was skinny, and probably weighed about the same as he did.

It stared at him curiously.

"I got no food. I'm hungry too," Miguel said. "Go away."

The dog wagged its tail.

Miguel turned his back on it to continue scavenging. For the past few days neither his parents nor his sister had found anything. The family was desperate. He had to find something, anything, that could be sold so they could eat.

The dog hung around. It watched Miguel scrabbling through the garbage, not moving any closer or farther away.

"Whaddaya want?"

Miguel stopped moving his hands. It was hard to concentrate under that gaze.

"You got a problem?"

The dog drew closer, and Miguel tensed. He'd heard about wild dogs attacking children. But the dog did not pounce. Instead, slowly but full of confidence, it walked right up to him. Then it started sniffing around where Miguel had been rustling through the garbage.

"Nothing to eat there," Miguel said.

He thought the dog must be hungry, like him. It began turning over garbage with its front paws. It looked over at Miguel as if to say, *I can do it.*

"You gonna help me?" Miguel asked.

At the sight of the dog steadily digging through the garbage, Miguel felt a sudden bond with it.

"Okay. Let's work together."

Miguel resumed scavenging. He'd already turned over every piece of trash in sight and found nothing of value. Still, he kept on digging as if in competition with the dog. Though he was doing the same old thing, it was somehow a lot more fun to be doing it with a dog.

3

Miguel took Tamon for a walk near a shopping mall. After emptying his bladder and bowels, Tamon fell into step with Miguel. The leash never strained or became slack. They had been walking for about twenty minutes when Tamon turned around at the sound of voices behind them. A group of children were on their way home from school.

"You like kids?" Miguel asked.

Tamon looked straight ahead again.

"If you go south, will you find the kid you're looking for?"

Tamon gave no response. Miguel shrugged. He pulled out his phone as he walked and made a call.

"Did you find out what happened to Ricky and Jose?" he said without preamble when the call was answered.

"Both dead. The cops are after you, too, not just Takahashi and his gang."

"That so? There was a driver, a Japanese guy. Is he alive?"

The fact that the cops were looking for Miguel meant somebody had squealed on him. Since Jose and Ricky were dead, it could only be the driver.

"He was found alive but died in the hospital."

"I see."

"He was probably the one who squealed on you to the cops."

"Got it. I'll be in touch."

Miguel hung up. He pulled down the brim of his baseball cap to cover his eyes.

"I knew he was done for."

Tamon looked up and met Miguel's eyes. Miguel saw his face reflected in them, eyes so deep and black he felt he might drown.

"You knew, didn't you?" Miguel muttered.

Dogs could sense things that humans couldn't. Miguel knew that dogs could put this ability to use in many ways.

"Looks like I'm your family now," he said.

Tamon set off walking again, straight ahead.

You want me to have a thief be my family?! Miguel imagined Tamon thinking. Miguel scratched his head.

A POLICE CAR APPROACHED in the oncoming lane. Miguel tightened his grip on the steering wheel. He knew the Miyagi cops were searching for him, but Fukushima police should be safe enough. This didn't make him any less nervous, though. If the cops pulled him over for a routine check and found the suitcase in the back, it was all over. When the patrol car disappeared from the side-view mirror, he heaved a big sigh of relief.

Miguel checked the rearview mirror. Tamon had his face turned to the left, or south. Miguel knew he was lucky that a dog as smart as Tamon had chosen to be with him. But whomever Tamon was looking for was obviously irreplaceable to him.

"I'll make you forget."

The traffic light ahead changed from yellow to red. Miguel stepped on the brake. Behind him, a Mercedes-Benz wagon that had already turned left at an intersection suddenly braked and made a U-turn. Miguel observed it in the side-view mirror with narrowed eyes. The traffic light turned green. He stepped on the accelerator and crossed the intersection. The Mercedes followed him, four cars back.

"Shit," Miguel cursed.

Takahashi and his gang had identified his car. The dealer he got it from, a guy who also sold stolen cars to Russians and Middle Easterners, must have leaked the description.

Miguel sped up and forced the car in front of him to let him pass. The Mercedes did the same. There was no mistaking it:

yakuza groups with links to Takahashi were on the lookout for his car.

"Hang tight, Tamon. This might get a bit rough."

Miguel went faster. At the next intersection the light changed from yellow to red, but he sliced through without slowing down.

Car horns blared. The Mercedes stopped at the light.

MIGUEL CALLED THE DOG Shogun. He liked the ring of this Japanese word that he'd heard somewhere.

Shogun appeared out of nowhere every morning, worked hard all day scavenging through the garbage alongside Miguel, then disappeared at sunset. Miguel wanted Shogun to live with him but knew his parents wouldn't allow it. He was also afraid of his father wanting to eat Shogun. Life was that tough. Shogun seemed to understand, though.

"Your nose is good, right? Find me something to make us a heap of money. Then Mama and Papa might let you live with us."

Miguel often spoke to Shogun while scrabbling through the garbage. With Shogun at his side, Miguel's loneliness was eased and the long, tedious days were a little more bearable. Shogun became like family to him, and Miguel could not imagine a world without the dog.

At noon, Miguel would take a break from work and find

somewhere out of the sun to play with Shogun. It helped distract him from the unbearable hunger.

One day Miguel was messing around with Shogun, as usual. But after a little while Shogun lost interest and started sniffing around the area.

"What's up, Shogun? You smell food?"

Miguel tracked Shogun's movements. Shogun had once found a small packet of cookies. Soggy, maybe, but still edible. Miguel never forgot the sweet taste on his tongue. His stomach rumbled at the thought. His mouth salivated.

Shogun stopped searching and began digging in one spot with his front paws.

"Is that where the food is?"

Miguel raced over to Shogun and began digging with him. After a while his fingers touched paper. Oilpaper, wrapped around some kind of heavy object.

"Hey, what's this? It's not food."

Miguel pulled a long face as he picked up the object with both hands. The paper peeled away.

"Mamma mia," he said with a gulp.

It was a gun. No shit.

"Shogun, this is worth money," Miguel said.

He gripped the gun in both hands and pointed it in the air.

"We can sell this for cash. Papa will know where. Now Mama and Papa will let you live with us."

Shogun wagged his tail.

"Let's go. We'll find Papa and show him. I'll tell him you found it."

Miguel wrapped the gun in the oilpaper again and hurried away. Shogun followed behind him.

Happiness bubbled up inside Miguel's chest. Spontaneously, he opened his mouth and laughed aloud.

MIGUEL LEFT THE BAN-ETSU EXPRESSWAY at the Aizuwaka-matsu city exit.

He knew that after his encounter with the Mercedes at Koriyama, the yakuza would be on the lookout for him on regular roads. He'd be safer getting on and off the expressway until reaching Niigata. He also wanted to get a different car but had to wait until nightfall to steal one.

Avoiding the main highways, he traveled west and pulled up on the edge of the parking lot at a roadside station just before the Agano River. Miguel let Tamon out of the car, and they walked around for five or so minutes while Miguel scanned for suspicious activity.

"You can exercise as much as you like after dark," Miguel told Tamon, and shut him up in the car again with food and water.

Then he went and got himself a pork cutlet with sauce over rice and quenched his thirst with a canned coffee from a vending machine before returning to the car.

He lay down in the back seat. "Wanna come up here?" he called to Tamon in the back.

Tamon looked at Miguel.

"Come on," Miguel said, and Tamon nimbly scrambled over the seat rest onto the back seat. He curled up and snuggled into the narrow space between Miguel and the seat back.

Miguel rested his hand on Tamon's back. He could feel his warm body under his soft fur. It wasn't long before Tamon was snoring. When the car was in motion he was always awake, searching for signs in the south. But even sitting in the car he would be using up energy. Miguel knew the dog would be tired.

"Do you forgive me, even a little?" Miguel asked Tamon.

There was no response, and Miguel smiled wryly.

"I'm not family, am I? Not even one of your pack. Was that Japanese guy the same? Just someone you met on the road? Your real pack is down south."

Miguel closed his eyes.

"But you're not going south. You're coming to Niigata with me. We'll get a boat there. You'll be *my* family."

Tamon's body shook. His hind legs twitched. Miguel opened his eyes. Tamon was dreaming. Dogs, too, had dreams.

"What did you dream of? Meeting your pack again? Dream on. You're mine now."

Miguel gently stroked Tamon's back.

"Sorry, Tamon."

Miguel closed his eyes once more and gave himself up to the sandman.

MIGUEL WAS AWOKEN BY the noise of a loud engine. It was night, and a full moon had risen high in the sky.

Miguel sat up and strained to see through the window. There were still many cars in the lot. He saw the source of the noise: a black sedan backing into a space near the shop and the restaurant.

Tamon stirred. He sensed Miguel's alertness.

"It's okay," Miguel said.

The engine cut, and the car's headlights went dark. Three men got out of the sedan. They were clearly not your average citizens.

"Here comes trouble."

Miguel watched them closely as he reached for the suitcase. He'd been wrong in thinking he had a bit of time. Takahashi was evidently desperate to get his hands on the money.

"Even yakuza get in deep shit over money . . ."

The men split up. Two went inside the building, and the other went around checking vehicles in the lot. He didn't even glance at sedans or light cars. Obviously he'd been informed that Miguel was driving a Volkswagen SUV.

"Quiet," Miguel ordered Tamon.

He reached under the seat and opened the toolbox. Arming himself with a wrench, he got out the car. The man whistled as he drew closer. Miguel circled around and hid in the shadows of a mini truck diagonally opposite. It was only a matter of time before the man noticed the Volkswagen.

"What have we here?"

The man stopped in front of the mini truck. He was staring at Miguel's car.

On tiptoe Miguel crept up behind him and brought the wrench down on the back of his head. The man gave a short yelp and crumpled on the spot. Miguel tossed the wrench aside and put his arms around the man. He dragged him over to the passenger side of the Volkswagen and lifted him into it.

Tamon growled at the unconscious figure.

"Wait," Miguel said, and shut the door.

He made his way over to the sedan, keeping to the dark of the shadows. The two other men were still inside the building. Miguel took his knife from his pocket, unfolded the blade, and slashed both rear tires of the sedan.

He scurried back to the Volkswagen, grabbed the suitcase, and let Tamon out. Tamon's eyes swept the area. He was poised and ready to move.

"Attaboy, Tamon. You look like a wolf." Miguel smiled.

With Tamon's leash in his left hand and the suitcase in his right, Miguel put the roadside station behind him.

4

When they reached National Route 4 on foot, the roar made the silence they'd left behind seem like a dream. Trucks rumbled along the blacktop in a cloud of vibration and noise that shook the night.

After crossing the Agano River, Miguel had initially chosen a less trafficked road to head west on. His plan was to get hold of a new car along the way, but he couldn't find a single vehicle in the fields that surrounded them. After two hours of fruitless searching, Miguel gave up and returned to the highway. The suitcase weighed heavy on his right arm. He needed rest but first wanted to get as far away as possible from this town.

"How you doing, Tamon?"

Miguel was exhausted, but Tamon's step was as firm as ever. He had Miguel's back and was keeping a close watch over their surroundings. Tamon was ready to do what needed to be done in order to protect his pack from outsiders.

Whenever a westbound truck approached, Miguel lifted his right arm to thumb a ride. Nobody stopped, but he kept trying anyway.

Finally, one truck pulled over. "Where you going?"

The driver was not Japanese. He looked Middle Eastern, with his beard and light brown skin.

"Niigata," replied Miguel.

"I go as far as Uonuma. If that's okay, you can ride with me."

The driver shot Tamon a tender look. He had stopped for the dog, not Miguel.

"Uonuma is good," Miguel replied.

With the driver's help, he loaded the suitcase and Tamon into the passenger side of the cabin. Miguel got in last.

"I am Hami. You?"

"Miguel."

Miguel shook the hand that Hami extended.

"Do you speak English?" Hami asked in fluent English.

"No problem," Miguel replied in English.

"What's the dog's name?"

"Tamon."

"Tamon . . . What does that mean?"

"Guardian angel."

"Nice coincidence. My name, Hami, means guardian angel in Persian."

"How does an Iranian come to be driving a truck in Japan?" Miguel asked.

"Because it's work. The trucking industry is short of drivers. Most of the time nobody cares if you're foreign or not. So long as you do a good job. What kind of work do you do?"

"I'm tired. Mind if I sleep?" Miguel asked, dodging the question.

"Ah, sorry. Get some sleep. I'll wake you when we get to Uonuma. Okay to pet Tamon?"

"Sure."

Hami reached out his left arm to stroke Tamon on the head. Tamon did not relax his guard but permitted Hami to touch him nonetheless. He never growled indiscriminately. A sign of strength in a dog.

"I've got a dog at home. A Shiba. My daughter pestered me into getting it, but dogs are great."

"That's for sure," Miguel replied curtly, and closed his eyes.

MIGUEL'S FATHER SOLD THE gun and bought meat and eggs with the money. For a brief time the family ate well. As a reward, Shogun was allowed to sleep with Miguel and given leftover bones and sinews to feed on.

For one week the family was happy. But it all ended when the men appeared. They were out for blood.

"Shhhh, Shogun." Miguel hid with Shogun in the shadows, watching as the men closed in on his mother and father inside the house.

"How did you get the gun? Where did you find it?" Miguel heard them demand.

"I . . . I don't know. My boy's dog found it."

His father's voice sounded muffled. He could hear his mother crying. His sister was nowhere to be seen.

"A dog found it? What shit is that? You trying to fuck with us?"

"It's the truth. I swear."

"Where's the kid and the dog?"

Miguel couldn't hear his father's reply. His mother's sobs grew louder. Miguel bit his lip. He wished he hadn't found the gun.

Suddenly, a shot rang out. His mother screamed. Again came the sound of gunfire, and his mother's screams stopped.

Miguel bit down on his hand to keep himself from crying out loud. Shogun gave a low growl.

"I said be quiet."

Miguel held Shogun back. He stole another look and saw his mother and father lying on top of each other.

Shot and killed.

It's my fault. My and Shogun's fault. I shouldn't have taken that gun. Miguel was drowning in grief, fear, and anger. He wished he had never found the gun.

"Find the kid and the dog. They have to be here somewhere."

The men fanned out. One headed in Miguel's direction.

"Shogun, whadda we do? They'll find us. We'll be killed too."

Shogun turned away from Miguel and looked back as if to say, *Follow me*. His ears stood up, and his tail was raised high. He looked full of confidence.

"Follow you?" Miguel asked.

Shogun raced off. Repeatedly he slowed down and looked back to check that Miguel was keeping up. Miguel concentrated on following Shogun. He thought he knew every corner of this garbage dump but was discovering that wasn't so. Shogun led him to places he'd never been before. They threaded through the garbage along tracks hardly wide enough to be called paths. The towering piles of trash on either side hid them from the men's view.

"Shogun, wait. I can't run anymore."

Miguel was panting and tripping over his own feet. How far had they gone? He stopped and crouched down on the spot.

Shogun came back and stood in front of Miguel. He stared

dumbly at him, waving his upright tail in an exaggerated motion.

"Okay, I get it."

Miguel stood. Shogun started running again, and Miguel followed. His lungs burned. Beads of sweat trickled into his eyes and stung them. Miguel didn't know where he was anymore.

Then all of a sudden the view opened up. They had left the garbage dump and were now in town.

Shogun increased his pace. Miguel could not keep up.

"Wait, Shogun. You're too fast."

As soon as Shogun disappeared from sight, Miguel became frightened. His mother and father were dead. He didn't know where his sister was. He was all alone.

"Shogun!"

Miguel stopped running and began to cry. Passersby looked at him, but nobody stopped to ask what was wrong. In this town, no one could afford to look out for anyone other than himself. It was that kind of place.

"Miguel!"

Miguel looked up upon hearing his big sister's voice. Shogun was running toward him, with Angela following behind.

"Angela!" Miguel cried. In that moment she appeared to him like a goddess and Shogun the angel who served her.

"What's wrong, Miguel? Shogun suddenly appeared and was biting my skirt. I wondered what happened and followed him."

Miguel threw his arms around Angela. "Papa and Mama are dead," he sobbed.

"What?"

Angela went still. Shogun looked up at Angela and Miguel.

change in the truck's movement roused Miguel from his sleep. Hami was maneuvering the truck into the parking lot at a convenience store.

"Sorry. Desperate to use the bathroom."

Once he'd parked the truck, Hami hurried inside.

It was still dark. Miguel noticed several cars in the lot.

Tamon, who was curled up at Miguel's feet, lifted his head.

"You wanna take a pee too?" Miguel asked.

Tamon had not had any food or water since the roadside station. He was bound to be hungry and thirsty.

Hami came back.

"I'm taking the dog for a pee," Miguel said to him. "Sorry, but could you get me some dog food and water while I'm gone, and paper bowls too?"

He handed Hami a 10,000-yen bill.

"Sure, happy to."

Miguel got Tamon down and walked him around the convenience store. Tamon seemed satisfied with stopping twice to pee on utility poles.

When they returned to the truck, Hami was in the driver's seat eating a rice ball. "Here's your stuff." He handed Miguel a plastic bag through the window. The receipt and change were inside.

"Take this," Miguel said, and tried to give him another 10,000-yen bill.

Hami refused. "I didn't pick you up for the money," he said.

Miguel gave Tamon the food and water. He drank some water himself and smoked a cigarette. When Tamon was done eating, Miguel threw the bowl in the trash and they returned to the truck.

"Ready to go?"

Miguel nodded, and Hami maneuvered the truck.

"Have something to eat. I bought some for you too."

Hami pointed to the plastic bag on the dashboard. Inside was a rice ball and bottle of black tea.

"Thank you," said Miguel, but he made no move to reach for it.

"Excuse me for asking something," Hami said after a while.

"What?"

"Did you steal the dog too?"

Miguel turned to look at him. "What are you saying?"

"You didn't answer my question earlier about what kind of work you do. Because you are a criminal. I know your kind. You're carrying either stolen goods or money in that suitcase. That's why you were so generous with the ten thousand yen. It's why I asked if you stole the dog too. He doesn't seem used to you, and you don't have any dog food with you."

Miguel put his hand in his pocket and gripped the handle of his knife.

"Don't get me wrong," Hami said. "I don't know who you are. After I drop you off at Uonuma, we're done. I won't notify the police. The reason I picked you up is the dog."

"I didn't steal him," Miguel replied. "The owner died, so I took over looking after him."

"Did you kill the owner?"

Miguel shook his head.

"That's okay, then." Hami nodded.

Miguel loosened his grip on the knife.

"You plan on boarding a ship in Niigata, don't you? The dog going with you?"

"There are ways," Miguel answered. He assumed Hami was referring to quarantine regulations.

"Tamon always faces left. He was like that the whole time you were asleep. At first I thought he was keeping watch, but I don't think so now. It's like he's facing south. Whenever we stop at a traffic light, he screws up his nose and sniffs the air."

"You're right. This one always knows where south is."

"He must have family in the south," Hami declared firmly. "When I was a kid we had dogs. My family had sheep. We couldn't have made a living without dogs to help round up the sheep."

Miguel stretched out a hand to pat Tamon, who was sitting at his feet. As usual, Tamon's nose pointed south.

"One day when I was little, I wanted to go into town and wandered off without telling my family. But I was small, and it got dark before I arrived. So I curled up on the side of the road and started crying. I could hear animals howling and was so scared, but there was nobody around. I cried all night until it was almost dawn, and then my father appeared with the dog. After I disappeared, it had been pointing in the direction of town and barking the whole time. So my father knew that's where I had been going and came looking for me. Dogs can sense these things."

"I know," Miguel said.

Shogun had led him straight to Angela. He didn't follow a scent trail or anything; he just knew where Angela was.

"Whoever is down south must be very important to this dog."

"You trying to tell me something?"

Hami shrugged. "You might be a criminal, but you don't look rotten to the core to me. That's what."

"He's my guardian angel," replied Miguel.

"He might be somebody else's guardian angel too."

"Why are you sticking your nose into what's none of your business?"

"Because I feel sorry for the dog."

"Sorry?"

"A dog needs family, not a traveling buddy. A member of its own pack. You're not that person."

"I need family too," Miguel said.

Hami smiled sadly but said nothing more.

Once they were out of the city, both sides of the highway were hidden in deep darkness. The truck's headlights sliced through the night. There was not another vehicle in sight, ahead or behind.

In his mind, Miguel saw an image of a lone truck plowing through the darkness on the road to the land of the dead. Riding in the truck was himself, an Iranian stranger, and a dog he had just met.

It had always been this way for him. After their parents were killed, Angela and Miguel switched from scavenging garbage to stealing. They couldn't have survived otherwise. And Miguel began making a name for himself as a thief.

"Mind if I smoke?" Miguel asked Hami.

"I don't mind, but if you really value that dog, it'd be better not to," Hami said.

Miguel had already been reaching for his cigarettes but drew back his hand.

"I've got gum, if you want."

"I'll have a piece."

"I knew you weren't all bad," said Hami, looking pleased.

ANGELA AND MIGUEL'S NEW home was a broken-down car abandoned on the outskirts of the city.

They had no desire to return to the garbage dump, and even if they had, the two of them wouldn't have been able to survive on their own there. They didn't know how to turn any finds into cash. Their father had always been the one who handled that.

Instead, they went every morning to the bustling city market. Angela looked for opportunities to pickpocket. Miguel stole fruit and meat. Then they would light a fire in the shade of the broken-down car and cook any fish or meat they had stolen. Without salt or pepper, the food didn't have much taste. But they were simply eating to live. Shogun showed them how.

Shogun was a first-class hunter. He brought them things

from out of nowhere. Miguel was not nearly as fast or reliable at getting them food.

If it hadn't been for Shogun, Miguel and Angela most likely would have starved to death.

Before long, Angela was calling Shogun their guardian angel. It was Shogun who found them the abandoned car, and Shogun who kept guard while they slept. Whenever police came around on patrol, Shogun alerted them. Miguel and Angela would jump out of the car and hide until the police were gone.

Every ounce of Shogun's strength was poured into protecting Angela and Miguel.

At first, Miguel resented Shogun. If Shogun hadn't found the gun, his parents would still have been alive. But he couldn't keep holding a grudge against the dog, who gave his all for them. Shogun simply did his best for Miguel and Angela. He expected nothing in return. He was filled with pure love.

The tragedy of his parents' death was a bitter blow to Miguel, but joining forces with Angela and Shogun to survive gave his days a sense of purpose. It was a different kind of life compared to mindlessly foraging through trash day after day. Miguel had to think, to work out how to steal without people noticing. Also how to hide out in the car without attracting attention. He enjoyed having to use his brain and making new discoveries.

Miguel was always hungry and never got enough sleep. But he survived. Angela loved him, and he loved Angela, and together with Shogun they battled on.

A year had gone by when Shogun showed signs of something being wrong with him. Miguel was the first to notice.

Shogun had brought Miguel and Angela a chicken. They cooked it over a fire and gave Shogun the bones. But that day Shogun didn't even look at his food. He lay slumped on the ground, breathing roughly, his face drained.

"Angela, Shogun's acting strange. He's not eating," Miguel said.

Angela stroked Shogun's back. "You're right. He doesn't look well."

"Whadda we do? He needs a vet."

"We can't afford it," Angela murmured sadly.

Angela understood. She knew Shogun was dying. But Miguel could not accept it.

"I'll get the money."

"Don't be silly. How much do you think it costs?"

"But we have to do something. Wait for me, Shogun."

Miguel set off at a run toward the market. His thieving skills had improved greatly in the past year, and he was now a much better pickpocket than Angela. He would find somebody who looked wealthy and steal their wallet. Then he could take Shogun to a vet.

Life without Shogun was unimaginable. It was only because of him that this existence was bearable.

Miguel spotted a target. A fat, middle-aged man wearing an unbuttoned shirt over a tank top, with a wallet peeking out from the back pocket of his jeans. His neck and wrists were ringed in heavy gold jewelry. He looked likely to be carrying lots of cash.

Miguel inched closer, waiting for his chance. When the man stopped to talk to an acquaintance, Miguel slipped the wallet from his jeans pocket. As he was about to run off, he felt himself grabbed by the shoulders.

"What are you doing with my wallet, punk?"

Before Miguel could sputter an excuse, the man punched him. He showed no mercy. Miguel was kicked, punched, and thrown to the ground. Even after he gave up the wallet, the man wouldn't stop. Before he knew it, Miguel found himself lying in a corner of the market.

Nobody went to the aid of the young boy covered in blood.

When Miguel eventually pulled himself to his feet, pain shot through his entire body. His head was throbbing. He dragged himself on shaky legs back to Shogun and Angela, who were waiting in the broken-down car. Somehow he made it.

"Sorry, Shogun. Sorry, Angela."

Angela was crying.

"Angela . . . ?"

A cold, heavy lump formed in the pit of his stomach. Forgetting his pain, Miguel ran to his sister.

Shogun's eyes were closed. He wasn't moving.

"Shogun?"

Miguel shook the dog. But Shogun was dead.

6

"The next day Angela started selling her body for money. With Shogun gone, it was hard for us to scrape together enough to eat," Miguel said.

"But Angela was still only a child, ten or so, wasn't she?" Hami's voice shook.

"There are perverts everywhere who like little girls. Just as many like little boys. I would've sold myself, too, but Angela wouldn't let me."

The eastern sky was beginning to brighten. As always, Tamon faced south.

"So that's how you came to be a professional thief."

"There was a boss man who rounded up kids like me and sent us out to steal. I depended on him."

Hami sighed. "Shogun was a real protector to you and your sister, true to his name."

"If it wasn't for Shogun, we'd have been dead a long time ago."

Miguel tossed a piece of gum into his mouth. Whenever he

felt like having a cigarette, he chewed gum instead. At this rate, maybe he could manage to quit.

"Did you get another dog after Shogun?" asked Hami, now totally absorbed in Miguel's life story.

"I wanted to but couldn't. I was always on the move, from town to town, country to country. I haven't seen Angela in years."

Miguel chewed on his gum, wondering how he came to be telling Hami his life story. He couldn't remember. He'd begun speaking before he knew it.

At least Hami was a good listener.

"I think you need to make a clean start," Hami said.

"Why do you say that?"

"The dog. If you turn over a new leaf, you'll be able to settle in one place. I say you plan to find somewhere to live with the dog."

"We were in Fukushima and Miyagi the last few months. It was like stealing from a corpse. I've had enough."

"Allah will bless you."

"I'm Christian."

"No matter. You will stop this life of crime. That would make me happy too."

"But we only just met."

"That doesn't matter. We are already brothers."

Miguel spat out the gum and wrapped it in a piece of paper.

Jose and Ricky, too, had been like brothers to him, and they were both dead. There were others before them whom he'd sworn brotherhood to, and they were also no longer in the world.

Everybody died. Only Miguel stayed alive.

People whispered behind Miguel's back, calling him a jinx or the god of death.

The older men warned younger ones against teaming up with Miguel, lest they risk death. Miguel had been turned down more times than he could count.

He believed it was his fault that Shogun, too, died. He was a jinx. That was why he needed a guardian angel.

Miguel was conscious of Tamon's eyes on him. Reading the secrets of his heart.

"You're all right," Miguel said to him, stroking Tamon's head.

"You leaving Japan for good?" Hami asked.

"Yeah. I'll go back and live with Angela. She's got a daughter."

"What's her name?"

"Maria."

"Good luck to Maria," Hami sang. "I'm sad to part so soon when we've only just become brothers."

"That's life," replied Miguel. "But the bond will still be there, no matter how far apart we are."

"You're right. We are brothers forever."

Hami extended his left hand. Miguel hesitated a second, then took it. Hami was neither a thief nor a criminal. He wasn't likely to die by becoming a sworn brother to Miguel.

"You don't happen to know someone who could sell me a used car, with no paperwork or other hassle, do you?" Miguel asked.

MIGUEL CLIMBED DOWN FROM the truck, picked up the suitcase with his right hand, and gripped Tamon's leash in his left.

"If you wait till night, I can take you to Niigata. You won't need to waste any money."

"Thanks, but I'll be okay from here."

Hami knelt down to hug Tamon goodbye, then stood up.

"Take care of yourself, then."

"If you have any reason to visit my country, please get in touch."

Miguel embraced Hami. Before getting out of the truck, they had exchanged addresses.

"*Xodâhâfez,*" said Hami.

"What's that mean?"

"Sayonara, in Persian."

Miguel nodded and watched Hami get back in the truck.

"Adiós, amigo," Miguel said when Hami leaned out the window to wave.

Hami smiled. "Be well, my brother," he responded in Japanese.

The truck pulled away.

Hami had dropped Miguel off at a convenience store on the outskirts of Uonuma. Miguel was to meet the car dealer at ten but could easily fill the time eating breakfast and walking Tamon.

"Okay, Tamon, let's get your breakfast first."

Miguel gave Tamon food and water. For his own breakfast, he ate the rice ball that Hami had given him.

Tamon wolfed down his food and immediately pointed his nose south, twitching it while sniffing the air.

"You really wanna find your friend, don't you?" Miguel said to him. "Can't I be your brother?"

Tamon didn't even look in Miguel's direction. With his nose pointed south and his eyes narrowed, he was fully focused on picking up a scent in the air.

"Good. That means you won't die."

Miguel unclipped the leash from Tamon's collar.

"Go," he said, and patted Tamon's rump. "Go find the one you have to protect."

Tamon raised his face to Miguel.

"It's okay. Go. You're free now."

Tamon walked away. After ten or so yards, he stopped and turned to look back.

"Go before I change my mind."

Miguel waved his hand as if to brush him away. Tamon took off. He ran with all his might, and in the blink of an eye he had disappeared into the distance.

"Adiós, amigo," Miguel said with a sigh. He threw away the leash.

ami turned up the volume on the TV with the remote control. His family was relaxing together after dinner. He and his wife were sipping coffee, and their daughter, Emi, played with Kenta, their Shiba.

"The body of an unidentified foreign national was discovered this evening at the north wharf in Niigata Port with multiple stab wounds to his body. Niigata police suspect the dead man belonged to a gang of organized criminals who carried out robberies in Fukushima and Miyagi Prefectures. Police are investigating."

No picture of the body was shown, nor was a name given. But Hami knew it was Miguel. Miguel was dead.

"Is anything wrong?" his wife asked.

Hami shook his head and switched off the TV. "It's nothing. I'm tired. I think I'll take a shower and go to bed."

"Good idea. You've got another early day tomorrow. You always work so hard."

Hami kissed his wife on the cheek and headed for the bathroom. The sight of Emi playing with Kenta overlapped in his mind with the image of Tamon.

Miguel was dead. But what about Tamon?

"Miguel would have let Tamon go his own way south," muttered Hami in Persian. Then he added, "Adiós, amigo."

iii

The Couple
and the Dog

1

W hat?" Taiki Nakayama stopped in his tracks. Something had leapt from the bushes a few yards ahead. Wild boar? Bear cub? The mother would be close by if that were the case. Dangerous too. Taiki didn't normally get spooked on the lonely mountain trails, but his heart was pounding.

The animal was looking all around and caught Taiki's scent. It turned to face him.

"A dog?" Taiki immediately relaxed. He was in no doubt. It looked like a German shepherd in shape and coloring, but smaller. Some kind of crossbreed, he guessed.

"What're you doing here?" Taiki asked the dog.

The dog lifted its ears ever so slightly. Its fur was dark around the mouth, with what looked like blood. Probably feeding on wild mice or something, Taiki thought. He could just make out a worn-out collar around the dog's neck.

"You a runaway, pooch? Must be hard to survive in the mountains."

Taiki pulled his water bottle from the side pocket of his backpack and drank. The trail was bathed in dappled sunlight slanting through the trees. It was hot and humid on the slope of Mount Ushidake. Taiki drove out here twice a week to train for trail running. He ran up to the peak and back on the mountain path.

The dog stared at Taiki as he drank his water.

"Thirsty?" Taiki asked.

The dog inched closer, as if it understood.

"Here, have some."

Taiki held his left hand to the dog's mouth and dribbled water into his palm. The dog deftly licked it up. As Taiki suspected, the black around its mouth was clumps of dried blood.

"Geez, you're scruffy," he said.

From its filthy appearance, Taiki guessed it had been wandering the mountains for quite some time since escaping from its owner.

"Hungry too?" He noticed its ribs were poking out.

After the dog had drunk, Taiki removed his backpack and dug out his supply of cookies. The dog wolfed them down.

"Must be hard hunting for food on your own."

When the dog had finished the cookies, it swung around to face in the direction of the trail ahead. Its nose twitched. Its eyes narrowed. Apparently it had picked up a scent.

"You smell food? Off you go and catch it. Bring it down. I'll say goodbye here."

Taiki picked up his backpack. He patted the dog lightly on the head and set off running again. Suddenly, the dog came racing up from behind, overtook him, then stopped ahead of him on the trail. It looked back over its shoulder, growling with bared fangs.

"What the—?"

The dog's growl was low and powerful. It began barking ferociously.

"Is this the thanks I get for giving you food and water?"

Taiki stopped running and steeled himself to be attacked. The dog kept barking.

"Give me a break," he said, scratching his head as he looked behind him. The peak was still forty minutes away. But if this kept up, he'd have to turn back early.

Again he looked at the dog. Though still growling, it didn't look as if it was preparing to attack Taiki.

"Hey, out of my way. I'm heading up."

Abruptly, the dog stopped barking and moved aside on the narrow path, seeming to have lost all interest in Taiki.

"Can I go now?" Taiki asked.

The dog did not react. Puzzled, Taiki set off running again. "Weird mutt."

Taiki's legs felt heavy. The unscheduled rest had affected

his rhythm. He took care to pace himself as he resumed running uphill. The trail continued straight for a while from the point where he had left the dog, then curved gently to the right. At the end of the curve, he stopped. In the middle of the path lay a black, steaming mass. Dung. From a wild animal.

"No way . . ." He could think of only one creature big enough to leave a dropping that size: a black bear. Had to be. The chances of encountering a bear face-to-face were low, but there were bears in these mountains.

Taiki could tell the dung was fresh because of the steam rising off it. He scanned the forest on both sides of the path but neither saw nor heard anything.

"If it hadn't been for that dog . . ." He looked back. The bear must've been scared off by its barking. "Enough running for today."

He turned and began to descend the trail. At the place where he had last seen the dog, he stopped. It was nowhere to be seen.

"Oy, pooch. You there?" he yelled into the woods. In the distance he heard the sound of dry grass snapping underfoot. Taiki braced himself.

"That you, pooch? Bark if it is."

He clenched his fist. When Taiki had first started trail running, he used to hang bear bells from his backpack and carry bear repellent spray. But he'd never had need to use the spray and after several years had stopped packing it. It was only extra weight he decided he could do without. The lighter the better was the general rule for walking or running in the mountains. So if there was anything he could to do reduce his pack in the slightest, he did it.

He heard footsteps approach. Too light for a bear. The thicket swayed and parted, then the dog leapt onto the path.

"You still here?" Taiki smiled at it. "All that barking before— you were scaring off a bear, weren't you? Did you smell it?"

The dog looked up at him with clear, unclouded eyes that hinted of a strong will.

"You saved my life. Wanna come with me? Be my dog and you won't have to worry about starving anymore."

The dog's tail swayed.

"Okay? It's a deal; you're mine. Let's go."

Taiki looked at the dog and set off running again. The dog followed, matching his pace to Taiki's.

Smart dog, thought Taiki. He guessed it'd been separated from its owner and was searching for him.

"Where's your master?" Taiki asked.

Not surprisingly, the dog did not respond.

'm home. I brought a new family member with me." Taiki's cheerful voice rang loud in the entrance hall.

Sae paid no attention and kept on working.

"I said I'm home. Don't ignore me," Taiki called even louder.

Sae tutted in annoyance and put down her tools. "Later. I'm finishing a stained-glass box I have to send this week."

"Come here, will you? I told you we have a new family member."

"A new family member?"

Sae stood up, looking mystified. She was aware of her face hardening into the expression that inevitably came over it whenever Taiki interrupted her unnecessarily. Massaging her cheeks with both hands, she made her way to the entrance hall. The skin on her makeup-less face felt rough and dry. When work was busy, she didn't have time for skincare.

"What are you talking about? New family—" Sae stopped midsentence and stared. Taiki held a rope in his right hand. At the other end was a filthy-looking dog.

"What are you doing with that dirty dog?"

"I was running on Ushidake, and this pooch saved my life. He chased a bear away. So I brought him home to thank him. That okay?"

Sae bit her lip. At least he was making a show of consulting her, but she knew that Taiki had no real intention of taking her opinion into consideration.

If Taiki decided to keep the dog, they would be keeping it.

"I'm gonna jump in the shower and then show my face at the store. Can you give the dog a bath, Sae? He's so dirty, my hand's black just from touching him."

"Hey, back up. I have to finish an order to send off this week, and—"

"Right, then you take care of it. I bought shampoo and supplies. They're in the car."

Taiki pressed the rope, or rather the leash, into Sae's hand and disappeared into the bathroom.

"He's got nerve." Sae glared in the direction of Taiki's back. She felt a tug on the leash and turned her attention to the dog. It was looking up at her. Composed and utterly unperturbed.

"You really are dirty, aren't you, fella? Are you lost? You seem very used to people."

Sae might have been angry with Taiki, but she melted at the dog's innocent gaze.

"Come here. I'll get you cleaned up."

She took it outside into the garden. The couple lived in a renovated eighty-year-old traditional wooden house with spacious grounds. Taiki had paved the area around the garage so he could have somewhere to tinker with his car.

It was a hot, cloudless afternoon, perfect weather for bathing a dog.

Sae hooked the leash over the mirror on Taiki's car.

"Wait here a minute."

She found dog food, dog pads, and shampoo in the back of the car, just as Taiki had said. A grubby object on the back seat appeared to be the dog's collar. Sae picked it up. There was a name tag attached, but the ink was so scuffed, she couldn't read it.

"This is no good. You have to have a name."

Sae grabbed the shampoo and shut the car door. She picked up the hose next to the garage and adjusted the head to shower spray. Usually it was set to jet, for washing the car.

"Have you ever had a shampoo?" she asked the dog.

It simply stared back at her.

"Don't be afraid. I'm going to wash you. You don't want to be dirty, do you? Dogs like being clean, don't they?"

Sae turned the lever, and water gushed from the hose. For a second the dog flinched, but it immediately recovered.

"Good boy. You trust me, don't you?"

She hosed the dog all over, and it quickly got soaked. The water dripping around its feet was pitch black.

"How long's it been since I washed a dog?" Sae muttered as she worked.

There had always been a dog in the house when she was growing up. Her father loved dogs, and it had been her job to wash them. But she hadn't looked after one since leaving home to go to college in Kanazawa.

"Must be more than twenty years . . ."

Sae bent over the dog and buried her fingers in its wet fur, moving them gently across its skin to massage it. She wanted to rinse off as much dirt as possible before shampooing it.

Water splashed on her T-shirt. The hem of her jeans got wet. Sae didn't care. She was planning to do laundry soon anyway.

"Next, shampoo."

She stopped the water and squeezed shampoo directly onto the dog's back. Once there was enough, she set to work rubbing with both hands to raise a lather. The dog patiently endured it.

"That's a good boy."

She peered into the dog's eyes and got a distinct sense of a powerful will behind them. The dog clearly did not like being shampooed but would put up with it if necessary.

"You trust people, don't you?"

There was too much dirt to work up a lather. Sae rinsed the dog again and applied more shampoo.

"Look at that, now you look nice. I bet you feel better too."

The stream of chatter she kept up was meant to relax him.

"Not very nice, is it, being taken to a complete stranger's house and given a wash without any say in the matter. But you put up with it all the same—you're such a good boy."

Once there were lots of bubbles, Sae stopped for a moment to examine the dog.

"Look at you, you're so thin and scrawny. Just skin and bones. When we're done here, I'll give you a big meal, all right?"

She rinsed off the shampoo. The water dripping off the dog's body was no longer black. Once the dog was rinsed clean, Sae brought several old towels out from the back of the garage and rubbed him down.

She used up three towels before water stopped dripping from the dog. Sae would have liked to use a dryer, too, but that would have meant going inside to get it and seeing Taiki, which she didn't feel like doing.

"Let's go for a walk. In this weather, you'll dry in half an hour."

Sae picked up the leash.

BY THE TIME THEY returned from their walk, Taiki's car was gone from the garage. Taiki had left for work. He had a sporting goods store, but despite low sales, he mostly left a casual worker in charge while he went trail running in the summer and ski mountaineering from the fall through the early spring.

The couple's main source of income was Sae's online business. She sold organic vegetables that she grew herself and stained-glass ornaments that she made by hand. The online shop had been going for only five years, but during that time her customer base steadily expanded through word of mouth. Sae had few business expenses and little overhead, and the year before last she had made more than 5,000,000 yen—a substantial income, enough for the couple to live on while paying off the house and car loans.

Taiki had become obsessed with trail running three years earlier. As soon as Sae's online shop took off, he lost interest in his own store and began spending half his week in the mountains.

Taiki was like a migratory fish. Keep moving, or sink. He'd always been that way. Cheerful and energetic, he didn't know the meaning of the word *shy*. He became friends with anyone within seconds of meeting them. This dog he'd dragged home was probably no different.

Sae wiped his feet with rags before letting him inside the house. Her mother had never liked having dogs in the house but had been overruled by Sae's father, who maintained that they, too, were members of the family and as such should be allowed indoors.

She placed the dog food on the table, poured some into a bowl, and put the bowl down in front of the dog. The dog sniffed at it eagerly but made no move.

"Are you being polite? Go on, you can eat," said Sae.

The dog began eating. In a flash the bowl was empty. He must have been ravenous.

Sae gave him some more. "That's all you're getting. No more after this. Too much food at once and your stomach will swell up. Then you'll be in trouble."

The second helping also disappeared in the blink of an eye. Sae ignored the plea in the dog's eyes for more. She spread a dog pad in a corner of the kitchen.

"So, apparently you live here now. Make yourself at home, but don't pee all over the place. This is where you do your business. I have to finish up some work and do the laundry, so I need to leave you on your own for a while. Understand?"

The dog raised his ears but yawned as soon as Sae finished speaking, as if bored.

Sae went to the bathroom and changed out of her wet T-shirt and jeans. She threw them in the washing machine with Taiki's running clothes and switched it on.

Upon returning to the kitchen she saw that the dog had moved to the living room. He looked cool and collected, as if he had always lived there, sprawled out next to the window, where he had a view outside.

"Are you keeping watch? Or looking for something?"

The dog lifted his ears when she spoke. That was all, though. Otherwise he stayed motionless, staring out the window.

"We have to find you a name," Sae said, but in her heart she had already decided. His name would be Clint, after the boxer that was the first dog she had ever known. Her father had been a Clint Eastwood fan. Clint had been an affectionate dog, and Sae's best friend.

"Right, then, I have to get back to work."

Clint, she called, without voicing the word. The dog looked over his shoulder. He wagged his tail, as if to say, *Gotcha*.

Sae felt a warmth deep in her heart. How could she have forgotten the joy of living with a dog? And all the love and happiness that a dog could give? She crouched down beside Clint and placed a hand on his back. His freshly shampooed fur felt soft. She was seized by the illusion that Clint had been living with them for years.

Then she lay on her side and slid her cheek against Clint's body. Clint accepted her touch without protest.

3

Sae was in the middle of soldering when her phone rang. Taiki. She clucked in irritation. Once her concentration broke, it was hard to get back into the flow. Time and time again she had asked Taiki not to call her during her work hours, but her requests went in one ear and out the other.

"Hello." Her tone was surly.

"Hi, it's me. I just got a call from Kazuaki. We're going out for a drink tonight, so I won't need dinner."

Kazuaki was one of Taiki's ski buddies. There was a whole bunch of them who went ski mountaineering in the Tateyama Ranges every winter.

"Taiki, do you remember that you brought a dog home today?"

"Of course. How could I forget? He saved my life."

"So the first night your savior spends in this house, you plan on going out drinking?"

"We've got important stuff to discuss." Taiki was unapologetic.

"But hasn't the ski season finished?"

"We don't just talk about skiing. Anyway, you're there, so the dog will be okay. You're used to dogs, aren't you?"

"Yes, but—"

"That's settled, then."

"Wait a minute—" Sae quickly jumped in as Taiki's voice grew distant.

"What?"

"We have to give the dog a name. I was thinking about it, and—"

"Tomba. I thought of it before. Good name, isn't it? Tomba, as in, you know, Alberto Tomba."

The name of a famous skier.

"But I—"

"Catch you later."

Taiki cut out before Sae could finish. It was always like this. Sae didn't even bother getting mad anymore. She looked down and saw that Clint had come to her side at some point.

" 'Tomba,' he said. You don't like that name, do you? Sounds like a pig." She stroked Clint's head. "Let's go for a walk and then have dinner."

Sae headed for the front door, and Clint followed. He understood they were going out. Sae could tell he was used to being around people. Even so, he seemed a particularly intelligent dog.

After attaching the leash to his collar, she opened the door. Outside, the faintly humid air caressed her skin. It was already past five o'clock, but there was still enough light for a walk. With summer approaching, the days were quickly getting longer. Once through the gate, they set out in the direction of the vegetable fields and rice paddies.

Although the couple's home was technically inside Toyama city limits, they lived in a tiny rural hamlet hemmed in on all sides by mountains. Their neighbors were all elderly, and children's voices were never heard. A little to the west lay the city of Nanto, and the border with Gifu Prefecture was slightly to the south.

Sae's parents also lived in Toyama city, but near the sea. Sae would have preferred to live by the sea rather than in the mountains, but Taiki was the opposite. Despite his all-around sporting image, swimming was not his forte. He was a stone in the water. *If we were by the sea and a tsunami came, I'd be dead*, he'd say. Three years earlier, whenever footage of the tsunami was shown on TV, Taiki would tremble in genuine fear.

Buying a house in the mountains had been Taiki's idea. Sae wasn't even consulted. It had been this way ever since they met. To all appearances, Taiki was a reliable, kind, athletic sort of guy. He was always smiling and not shy about anything, and he pulled Sae along in his wake.

Sae fell in love and accepted Taiki's marriage proposal, but it was only after they were married that she realized how shortsighted she'd been.

Taiki was indiscriminately kind to anyone and everyone. He made no distinction among his wife, friends, and complete strangers. But kindness was one thing; a complete lack of thought about actions and consequences was another. Even when it came to important decisions, Taiki did not give them deep consideration. He simply went with whatever his feelings were at the time. His take-charge attitude was not about looking out for others so much as getting his own way.

That was the kind of guy Taiki was. He wasn't a bad person. But he wasn't the kind of man to choose as a husband.

He wasn't a bad person. That was why Sae put up with him.

He's not a bad person . . . It was the one thing that gave her pause when she thought about divorce. It would be easier if he were an outright creep. Then she could have released herself from the spell of marriage a long time ago.

As Sae walked with Clint through the fields, she spotted an elderly woman hard at work pulling weeds. From the angle of the woman's bent back, she could tell it was Sumi Fujita, who lived three houses down. Sumi had taught Sae everything she needed to know about growing vegetables. Though almost ninety years old, she was still hale and feisty. Sumi straightened up when she noticed Sae and Clint approaching.

"Sae, dear, did you get a dog?"

Clint raised his ears but did nothing more. His composure, Sae guessed, stemmed from a confidence in being able to handle whatever situation arose.

"Taiki found him in the mountains. Apparently he chased away a bear."

Sae made her way along the path separating the fields to where Sumi stood.

"He looks like a smart one."

"He certainly is. He arrived only this morning, but it already feels like he's been living with us for years. I don't have to tell him a thing. He must have had a good owner. I can't imagine how they were separated."

"He's got a fine look about him."

Clint sniffed modestly at the hand Sumi extended.

"Would you like some steamed sweet potato? I brought some in case I got hungry out here, but at this age I don't have the same appetite I used to."

Sumi opened up a dainty pink waist pouch and pulled out the potatoes wrapped in foil. Clint's nose simultaneously began twitching.

"May I give him some?" Sumi asked Sae.

"Of course."

"It's from my own field. Not a drop of chemicals on it."

Sumi peeled away the foil, broke off the end of a potato, and brought it close to Clint's mouth. Clint gently took the piece and ate it.

"He's got good manners too." Sumi smiled broadly at Clint. She was impressed by his restraint and fed him several more pieces.

"There's a good boy. You really are a smart cookie."

When all the potato was gone, Sumi lightly stroked Clint on the head.

"Where's Taiki? He brought the dog home, didn't he? Has he gone off and left you to do all the work?"

Sae smiled bitterly.

"You need to shake a leg and leave that man. There's any number of men who'd appreciate you. I can look around for you, if you like."

"When the time comes, I'll let you know," Sae replied, laughing off Sumi's offer.

"He's not a bad person, but not the sort to make a woman happy. I can see it in his face. He must be nearing forty now. And still a child. He's just a kid who never grew up."

"Maybe . . . But he does have his good qualities."

"He barely does any work and is always off skiing or running in the mountains. That's fine for a bachelor, but not a married man." Sumi waved her hand across her face as if brushing away a fly. "If you don't leave him soon, Sae, you're the one whose life'll be ruined. What's this boy's name?"

"It's Clint," Sae replied.

"Like in a spaghetti Western. Clint, you're welcome to some more potato. And be a good boy and cheer up Sae here. Understand?"

"Thank you for the potato. We'll see you again soon."

"Ah, wait. There's something else I wanted to mention, Sae, dear."

Sae had already turned on her heels but stopped when Sumi called her.

"What's that?"

"I wondered if you'd like to take over the paddy next year."

"Your paddy, Sumi?"

Sae already had a half acre of rice growing on land she rented from the agricultural co-op. She harvested enough to feed her and Taiki for a year, to send gifts of rice to both of their families and a few friends, and to still have some left over. She had no need of a bigger harvest. Besides, growing organic rice was time-consuming and labor intensive.

"I don't have the energy anymore to grow rice," Sumi said. "But you sell vegetables on that internet, don't you?"

"Ye-es."

"Well, if organic vegetables sell, then rice could too."

There was truth in what Sumi said. Sae had already had inquiries from the customers who bought her vegetables, about buying organic rice as well.

"I could probably sell it, but my hands are full with just half an acre."

"Get that foolish husband of yours to help."

"He's busy with his own things."

"Busy having a good time, you mean? Anyway, think it over. It's hard work, but I can't bear to let the land go fallow."

"Yes, that'd be a shame."

If Sumi stopped growing rice, it meant she would stop weeding her fields. Untended fields had a knock-on effect. They quickly became overgrown and affected neighboring fields.

"I'll think about it," Sae said.

"That deadbeat husband of yours needs to shape up . . ." Sumi said as she turned away from Sae and Clint.

Sae suppressed a sigh at the sight of Sumi's back, which became more bent every year. "I'll be off, then," she called to Sumi.

Adjusting her grip on the leash, she walked off. Clint followed, matching his step to hers. He didn't make any sound. He didn't nod at what she said. He was simply there. Why was that so comforting? she wondered.

Sae looked down at Clint and smiled. Clint stared straight ahead and kept on walking.

4

'm home," Taiki announced quietly as he slid open the front door. The lights were out already. Sae must be in bed.

He had meant to come home earlier but lost track of time. Before he knew it, it was midnight, and he called the substitute driver service to bring him home.

Groping his way through the darkness, he tried not to wake Sae.

"Huh?" He could hear breathing. He froze.

Two white dots loomed in the darkness.

"Tomba?" Only now did he remember the dog. There was a faint scent of shampoo in the air.

When his eyes became accustomed to the dark, the outline of the dog emerged. It was standing in the middle of the hallway, looking at Taiki.

"Don't scare me like that. I almost had a heart attack."

They lived deep in the countryside. Wild animals getting into the house wasn't such a far-out notion.

Taiki went and grabbed the headlamp they kept on top of

the shoe cupboard in the entrance hall and switched it on. Tomba squinted in the glare.

"Look at that, you're all clean. I wouldn't have known you. Sae did a great job. I knew she would."

Taiki stroked Tomba's head and went into the living room. He threw himself down on the sofa. "Ugh, I drank too much . . ." he muttered while massaging his temples.

Tomba came over and lay down on the floor next to the sofa.

"Did you eat?" Taiki asked.

Tomba merely shot Taiki a quick upward glance.

"Come here. My lifesaver . . . I'll give you a reward."

When Taiki beckoned, Tomba stood up and leapt into the empty space on the sofa. Taiki pulled Tomba close. His fur was soft and pleasant to touch, a far cry from what it was like when Taiki had found him on the mountain.

"Sae's probably forgotten, but I always said to her before we got married that I wanted to get a dog one day. I'm such a slacker, I never got around to it, though. Then fate brought me you. Are you a gift from the gods, pal?" He gently rubbed Tomba's back.

Taiki knew Sae was frustrated with him. He had to admit he wasn't much of a husband. He was too occupied with other things. Trail running in summer, ski mountaineering in winter, and a hobby shop that hardly made any money. He knew he should work alongside Sae in the fields and help her out with shipping orders for her store. He knew it, but he couldn't do it.

He'd always skied, ever since he was old enough to remember. In high school he won the prefectural ski championship, and then gone on to the nationals. His ambition ballooned until it became his goal to compete in the Nagano Winter Olympics.

But in the winter of his last year at high school, he suffered a major injury. While going too fast down a slope, he fell with tremendous force. One ski spiked in a hard patch of snow, and his right leg took the impact, shattering his shin with a compound fracture.

After operations and physical therapy he was able to resume regular life well enough, but never able to return to top-level competition. Ever the optimist, Taiki rebounded from this disappointment with little difficulty. But he could not forget the thrill of skimming over a slope of packed snow at speed.

For him, there was no point skiing the slopes if he could not return to competition. Happily for Taiki, many of his ski buddies were into ski mountaineering. The sport entailed climbing a mountain with skis on your back and then skiing down. It soon had Taiki in its thrall. He started off with relatively easy thousand-meter mountains and gradually worked up to higher conquests.

Climbing mountains in winter required technical skill as well as strength. Taiki became infatuated not only with ski mountaineering, but with mountain climbing as well. So he began trail running in the mountains in summer to build up strength for the winter season. It wasn't long before he was obsessed with trail running too. There was nothing like the bracing sensation of running along high mountain ridges.

What had begun as part of a training regimen quickly became a pursuit in itself. After taking part in a few competitions, Taiki became hooked on the thrill of winning. It was what made him neglect work to head for the mountains and run.

If he wasn't moving his body somehow, he didn't feel alive. Being in motion on a mountain was the only thing that made him feel truly himself.

"Sae forgives me, so I can't help it."

Tomba stared hard at him.

A courtroom scene like he sometimes saw on the news unexpectedly came into his mind. The prosecutor and defense attorneys presenting their arguments while the judge listened intently. Tomba was like the judge. He listened to each side and handed down a judgment, without allowing personal feelings to interfere.

Am I guilty or innocent? Taiki smiled wryly. "I drank too much tonight."

He rose to his feet and went to the kitchen, using the head-lamp for light. He pulled a sports drink from the fridge. As he was closing the door, a semitransparent container caught his eye. It contained steamed sweet potato cut into bite-size pieces. Sae had probably cooked it for Tomba.

Tomba had followed him into the kitchen.

"Want some sweet potato?" he asked.

Tomba pricked up his ears and wagged his tail.

"Okay, then. It's late, so just a bit."

He counted out five pieces and gave them to Tomba. Tomba ate them and thrust his face under the dining table. One of the dog pads Taiki had bought was spread underneath the table with a ceramic bowl filled with water on top of it.

"Did Sae do this? She thinks of everything." Taiki drank the sports drink in one long gulp.

Sae did all the housework and earned money as well. Without grumbling or a word of complaint. But the way she looked at Taiki now was a lot different from when they were first married.

"I know," Taiki said to Tomba, who had finished drinking. "I know things can't go on like this. Even my trail running and ski buddies can't believe me. I'm the worst husband ever, according to them."

Taiki returned to the living room and sat down on the sofa

again. Tomba climbed up next to him and rested his jaw on Taiki's thigh.

"I know, Tomba, I know. Still . . ."

As he got closer to forty he'd begun to feel a definite decline in his strength. He needed to run twice as often to keep up the same level of fitness, and if he didn't get that exercise in, he got antsy. When running wasn't enough anymore, he began going to the gym as well.

Gradually, he'd become more neglectful of his store and spent even less time with Sae. He was aware that her attitude toward him was rapidly changing. That a rift was widening between him and the wife he loved. He knew he had to do something, he knew he had to change, but he didn't know how.

All he knew was a relentless sense of restlessness.

He wanted to aim high for as long as possible. But how long could he keep running in top-level competition?

"Just give me five more years, Sae. Then I'll quit. Please bear with me till then," Taiki mouthed in the direction of the room where Sae slept.

The voices of his buddies teasing him still rang in his ears. *Whaddaya mean, top-level running? Come off it, man. Do you think you're a pro?*

"Five years, Sae. I only need five more years. Then I'll help with the fields or anything else you want me to do."

Drowsiness overtook him. Taiki reached out to switch off the headlamp. In that moment before the light went out, he caught a glimpse of Tomba's face in the corner of his vision. Looking up at him like a judge. Taiki patted Tomba's head and closed his eyes. He fell asleep immediately.

5

Mornings were busy for Sae. From the moment her eyes opened, time slipped away. She rose before dawn to harvest lettuce and other leafy summer produce, to fill the constant stream of orders from her online store. Then she had to pack and ship the vegetables. In between, she prepared meals and took Clint for walks.

There was so much to do, she hardly had time to breathe. Her body complained, and she would have given anything for Taiki to at least prepare a meal or take Clint for a walk of his own accord. Instead, he rose after eight, clamored for food, and petted Clint but never offered to take him out.

Who do you think puts food on the table? Who is it thanks to that you can spend all your time on your hobbies? Sae was writing out shipping labels while her thoughts grew more and more bitter.

"I'll be off, then," Taiki had said that morning when he left for the store around eleven. He opened at close to noon and closed at six. Sae's long hours were the only reason he was able to run his store in this princely fashion.

A warm feeling on her thigh jerked Sae back to reality. Clint was pressing himself against her.

"Oh, sorry, Clint."

She put down her pen and laid a hand on Clint's back. Dogs were sensitive to changes in human moods. She didn't want him getting anxious because of her own irritation.

"I'm a bit on edge. Did I bother you?"

Clint lay down at Sae's feet with his face pointing outside. Sae had noticed that Clint always faced west. Southwest, to be precise.

What was in the west? Sae asked Clint the question many times but of course got no answer. Was it simply coincidence? Or maybe his home was in the west?

Sae had posted a photo of Clint on social media to try to find his owner. A dog as well-trained as he was undoubtedly had been loved by somebody. If he had become separated from his owner due to some mishap, that person would be frantically searching for him.

But she got no response. Not even a scrap of information that might offer some clue.

"Where did you really come from?" Sae said to Clint as he lay at her feet. His nose pointed west. Clint lifted his ears but didn't move.

Sae's phone rang. She reached for it automatically.

"Hello?"

"Are you the owner of Wind Country?" A woman's voice gave the name of Sae's online store. The voice was firm and youthful. She sounded like she was in her thirties.

"Yes, I am."

"I ordered organic lettuce and cucumbers from you, and they arrived yesterday."

Sae sensed hostility in her tone. She steeled herself. Clint rose to his feet and watched her.

"When I cut the lettuce, I found a caterpillar in it—a caterpillar!"

"I'm very sorry about that. Our vegetables are grown by organic methods in a pesticide-free environment. We inspect them after harvesting, but sometimes insects do get overlooked. This is all explained on our home page, which—"

"Do you not understand? There was a caterpillar, a caterpillar! Organic or not, you've got some nerve selling vegetables with bugs in them! What if I had eaten it?"

The more she spoke, the more hysterical the caller became.

"There's a warning on the home page that this can happen."

"Are you saying it's my fault? For ordering without reading the fine print?"

"No, I didn't mean to—"

"All I wanted was to buy quality, well-sourced vegetables. If I'd known there'd be a caterpillar in them, I wouldn't have ordered. I can't believe your attitude."

Sae wanted to yell at her that a caterpillar was nothing, that if she washed the lettuce before eating it, there wouldn't be any problem, but she restrained herself.

"I apologize. If you'd like, I can refund your money."

"Of course you should. Who wants vegetables with bugs? It's a scam taking money for them. A scam."

Sae's hand shook. She'd had some wild complaints before but had never been spoken to in such a high-handed manner. She felt like shouting back at the woman, and the words rose in her throat. Then her eyes met Clint's.

Help me, Clint, save me, she pleaded with her eyes.

Clint rested his jaw on Sae's thigh. Instantly the warmth relaxed her.

"I will return your money immediately. Please follow the instructions on the home page to receive a refund. I am sorry that you had an unpleasant experience."

"I'll never order from you again."

The line went dead.

Sae bit down hard on her lip as she stroked Clint's head.

"Thank you, Clint. If it weren't for you, I would've lost it. But you can't do that in a customer service business. No matter how awful the customer."

Clint lifted his head to lick Sae's hand.

Don't let it get to you, she could almost hear him saying.

"You're right. I have to pull myself together. I've got ump-teen things to do that can't wait."

Sae picked up her pen and went back to writing out shipping labels.

After a while the phone rang again. She checked the caller display with a thumping heart. It was Taiki.

"Hi, it's me."

"I know. What is it?" Her voice came out sounding angry.

"This weather's too good to waste, so I'm going for a run on Ushidake. Wouldn't mind hamburgers for dinner."

As usual, Taiki was oblivious to Sae's mood.

"As if it's not enough that I'm so busy that my left hand doesn't know what the right is doing, my husband, instead of offering to help, is apparently off for a fun run *and* wants me to make hamburgers for dinner."

"Huh? What's bugging you?"

"Nothing."

What Sae had once believed to be Taiki's innocence she now regarded as insensitivity. He was hopelessly unheeding of other people's feelings.

"You know I'm no good at mindless work. I'd like to help, but I can't."

"You are unbelievable. Watch what you say."

"My bad," Taiki said, not sounding sincere in the least.

Sae's anger mounted.

"Anyway, I'm off. Anything's fine for dinner."

The line cut off. Sae gripped the phone tightly and sighed.

"Why can't he say a single word of thanks or encouragement? Just one word. It'd make all the difference."

She covered her face. Suddenly she felt inconsolable. Tears rolled from her eyes. How could this be? When she used to love him so much? When they had married and sworn to be happy forever? She reached out to touch Clint. He was her only consolation.

"Thank you for being here."

She buried her face in Clint's fur and wept.

6

Tomba, here, boy," Taiki called as he flopped down on the sofa. Tomba loped over and jumped up beside him.

Taiki squeezed him in a hug and roughly stroked Tomba's head, back, and chest. Tomba looked happy and relaxed.

"What happened today? Sae's in a bad mood," Taiki asked. "She hasn't said a word to me since I got back. Not even the whole time I was eating dinner."

He looked in the direction of the bathroom. Sae was in the habit of taking a bath after washing the dishes.

"And she served boil-in-the-bag curry for dinner. She always cooks me dinner—no matter how busy she is. She makes a great beef curry. Simmers it slowly on the stove in thick gravy. We haven't had it in ages . . . No, no, that's not right—she made it last month."

Taiki grinned foolishly and scratched his head. "Sae's a real grouch these days. Does she bite your head off too?"

Tomba swayed his tail.

"I know she's not the sort of woman to take it out on a dog. She's probably tired. She works too hard."

Taiki was not being entirely forthright. He knew it was only because of Sae's unstinting effort that he could do his own thing.

"I try to be considerate, but maybe it's not enough?"

Tomba kept wagging his tail.

The heavy, strained atmosphere that pervaded the house whenever Sae was in a bad mood used to be unbearable. But with Tomba around, it was different somehow. Perhaps his tail stirred the stale air.

"Do you think I don't do enough? It's my weak point, you know, not being able to read people. But I just get caught up in my own stuff, that's all. What do you think I should do?"

Tomba jumped off the sofa. He crossed the living room to the doorway and stopped to look back.

"What? You want me to follow?"

When Taiki stood, Tomba continued into the hallway. Taiki followed him and caught up to him in the front entrance. Tomba was gazing up at the leash hanging from the wall.

"You wanna go for a walk? Come off it."

Taiki stood with both hands on his hips.

Abruptly, Tomba seemed to lose interest in the leash and made his way past Taiki back to the living room.

"What was all that about? You got something to say? Spit it out."

Puzzled, Taiki returned to the living room. Tomba lay curled on the sofa.

"What are you trying to tell me? Let's have it."

He sat down on the end of the sofa, careful not to tread on Tomba.

"You wanted me to see the leash, but you don't want to go for a walk? I don't get it . . . What's a dog doing giving a person quizzes anyway?"

Taiki did an imitation comedy routine with himself and laughed weakly.

"I really wish you could talk."

He petted Tomba. The same instant, a current of electricity seemed to course through him. "That's it . . . Lately Sae's been getting up in the dark to pick her vegetables. But I could take you for your morning walk instead of her. Is that it, Tomba?"

That was why Tomba had led him to the leash.

"I don't think you're that smart, but it's given me an idea. I hope it puts Sae in a better mood. Wait here."

Taiki went to the kitchen. He grabbed a can of beer and some steamed sweet potato and carried them back to the sofa.

After pulling the tab off the can, he tapped it against Tomba's nose.

"Cheers. Here's to Sae getting in a better mood."

He gulped down a mouthful of beer, then gave Tomba the sweet potato.

"This is your reward for giving me a hint. Starting tomorrow morning, walks are with me. I'll have to get up early."

Taiki laughed and knocked back the rest of his beer.

ae arrived home after working in the fields. Taiki and Clint were nowhere to be found. A few days earlier Taiki had announced out of the blue that he was taking Clint for his morning walk. Sae didn't expect this routine to last, but he was managing to keep it up for now. She was grateful to him for doing the morning walk, but it was so like Taiki not to think of feeding Clint afterward. In the end it was Sae who soaked the dog food in lukewarm water, washed out the water bowl, and refilled it. She didn't want Clint getting gastric trouble from dry food that expanded in his stomach after he drank.

In the beginning, Taiki had occasionally fed Clint, but he gave up when Sae warned him about dry food. "It's too much hassle," he'd said.

"Why is it a hassle? Cooking your meals is way more trouble. And his name's Clint, not Tomba."

Taiki persisted in calling him Tomba. Sae called him Clint.

Neither Sae nor Taiki cared that the other called the dog by a different name. Clint answered to both.

"That's the kind of couple we've become."

Sae poured warm water from the kettle over the bowl of dog food. It would soon cool, and within half an hour the food pellets would lose all shape and crumble. It occurred to her that love, too, was like that. In the last twelve years the love between her and Taiki had cooled and lost its shape. Things could never go back to how they were.

Tears welled in Sae's eyes. But the thought of letting herself get sad over Taiki only made her angry with herself and produced more tears.

She had chosen Taiki. She had only herself to blame. She didn't want to despise Taiki more than she already did.

Sae could not stop crying. She washed her hands, still dirty from the fields, and wiped away her tears with wet hands.

When was the last time she'd put on makeup? She couldn't remember. It felt like decades since she'd gotten dressed up, put on makeup, and gone out for the evening.

Sae went to the bedroom and sat down in front of her dresser. She stared in the mirror. Her hair was lank with sweat, and her face was dry. Though she had only just turned forty, the face she saw in the mirror looked sixty.

I have to do something. Sae rummaged through her makeup. She was looking for eyebrow liner and lipstick. The eyebrow pencil needed sharpening, but she couldn't find a sharpener. The lipstick was dry, the color long out of fashion.

Sae turned away from the mirror. It wasn't supposed to be like this. Marry the man you love and have a family. Wasn't that the way it was supposed to go? It was neither of their faults that they hadn't been able to have children. Nevertheless, they should have been able to continue being a smiling, happy couple.

Now the only time she smiled with any sincerity was when she was with Clint.

"Come home quickly, Clint. Please."

Sae hung her head.

8

We're going up a mountain today. Ushidake, where I found you," Taiki said, his hands on the steering wheel. He was tired of walking Tomba in the neighborhood. How some people could walk their dog along the same route every day, year after year, he would never understand. If the owner was bored, surely the dog, too, must be.

On the way, Taiki stopped at a convenience store for energy snacks. Never go up into the mountains without food, even for a short run. If the body's store of energy became depleted, a person could hit a wall and become hypoglycemic. In that state, it was hard even to move. That was why it was important to always carry a source of immediate energy replenishment. Taiki bought energy snacks for himself and jerky for Tomba. "Dogs need energy, too, Tomba," he said. Water was no problem—he'd brought some from home.

Taiki planned to combine Tomba's walk with a run. Since it wouldn't be a proper training session, he didn't need to prepare too much. He parked in his usual place, changed into his running shoes, and did some warm-up stretches. After ten minutes he was ready.

"Okay, let's go."

Taiki secured his backpack, gripped Tomba's leash, and set off running. Tomba trotted beside him, a picture of graceful motion, matching his pace to Taiki's. Taiki would have preferred to be hands-free but couldn't be sure that Tomba would follow, so he held on to the leash. Sae would never forgive him if he lost Tomba in the mountains.

"Good stuff, Tomba."

When they came to the trailhead, Tomba dropped behind Taiki. Here, the path was too narrow to run side by side.

Taiki adjusted the length of the leash as he ran. Though he knew this trail well, running it with Tomba was a whole new experience.

"What do you think? Feels good, right, Tomba?"

Tomba was smiling. A smile spread across Taiki's face too.

"Attaboy. Clean air. Fantastic, isn't it? Sae doesn't get trail running."

Taiki's heart, lungs, and legs were all in top form. His muscles made no complaint, even when he upped the speed of his usual training pace. His breath came faster. The higher he went, the steeper the gradient became.

Taiki held himself back from going even faster. If this were training, he would be giving his muscles more load. But today was a substitute for Tomba's walk. He grinned at himself. He knew he tended to get too serious when it came to exercise.

After thirty minutes he stopped. "Rest time, Tomba."

Taiki drank some water and let his breathing settle. Tomba, too, was breathing heavily, but he still looked unruffled. Taiki guessed that Tomba must have been wandering in the mountains for several weeks when they first met, given all the dirt on him. This dog was used to mountain country. It would take more than a run like this to wear him out.

"You want water too?"

Tomba looked up at Taiki. Taiki poured water into the lid of the water bottle and held it to Tomba's mouth. Tomba lapped it up loudly.

"You're a natural runner. Lucky you," he said, stroking Tomba's face.

When Taiki returned the water bottle to his backpack, he grabbed a citric acid tablet, thinking it would be enough of an energy recharge.

Tomba accepted some jerky and started chewing on it.

"You okay without the leash? You won't run off, will you?" It was a nuisance having to hold the leash while running. When Tomba finished eating, Taiki unclipped the leash and stuffed it into his backpack.

"We'll run another thirty minutes, then turn back. Sae might be worried."

Taiki tapped Tomba on the head and then set off again. Every ten paces he turned to check behind him. Tomba stayed close behind.

"Attaboy, Tomba."

don't believe it. Where could they be?"

Taiki and Clint were still not back. Sae had tried phoning Taiki repeatedly but could not get through. She tried their messaging app as well, but there was no reply.

"Has something happened?"

Unable to wait around doing nothing, she jumped in the car. There was no sign of them on any of the farm tracks or roads in the neighborhood. Nor had anyone out in the fields seen them either when she stopped to ask. Where could they have gone?

Her unease and irritation mounted. If anything happened to Clint, she would never forgive Taiki. Her hands tightened on the steering wheel. She was astonished at herself for even thinking this. If they had gotten into an accident, then it wouldn't be just Clint who was hurt. Taiki might be hurt too. But there was a part of her that was okay with that, just as long as Clint was fine.

How could it be that a dog who'd lived with them for barely

a month was more important to her than the husband she'd spent more than ten years of her life with? Sae pulled over to the side of the road. She slumped back against the seat and closed her eyes.

"That's it. We're finished," she murmured, and bit her lip.

10

The view ahead opened out to reveal a scree slope. The trail at this point was even narrower and littered with rocks and boulders of all shapes and sizes. It ran along a ridge where a cliff fell away to the left. Any mishap here could mean a fall of nearly fifty meters.

Taiki slowed his pace and took care to avoid loose stones. "You take care, too, Tomba," he called over his shoulder. Tomba's rhythmic breathing came in reply.

During their first rest break, Taiki had decided to continue for another thirty minutes and then turn back. But he'd become so absorbed in running that nearly an hour had passed. He decided to cross the scree and then take another break. Tomba, too, would be tired.

The temperature was rapidly climbing. Perspiration ran down Taiki's body. His throat was parched. His right inner thigh started to cramp, probably from sweating too much.

"I overdid it, went too fast," Taiki muttered. When he was younger he'd been able to ignore day-to-day changes in his condition, but he couldn't afford to do that now. Not only were the ups and downs in his performance more extreme, but even on a good day he could run out of energy all of a sudden if he went too fast.

"Water and a supplement at the next break," he decided. The cramp would ease up if he took one of the amino supplements he kept in his backpack.

The end of the scree lay a few hundred feet ahead. He would rest there.

"Just a little longer, Tomba. We'll run just a bit farther and then rest before turning back."

Taiki could see where the trail entered the forest ahead. *Just a bit farther*—in that moment, Tomba suddenly barked behind him.

"What is it?"

Taiki turned to look behind him, and an image of the first time he had seen Tomba flashed through his mind. "Bear?"

His knees went weak at the thought of encountering a black bear. He decided to stop. But as he went to brace the muscles in his legs to control his momentum, his right thigh cramped.

"Ouch!" His face screwed up in pain as he balanced on his left leg. The stone under his foot was loose, and his footing became unsteady.

No! he thought, losing his balance. His body tilted to the left while his right leg jutted out in the air. Desperately he stretched out his arms, but his hands found nothing to clutch on to.

He cried out for help. "Tomba!"

It was futile. Taiki fell from the cliff with the names of his loved ones on his lips.

"Tomba, Sae—"

His body struck hard against something, and he lost consciousness.

11

A t the heliport, uniformed men climbed down from the mountain rescue helicopter. They pulled out a stretcher and walked it toward Sae.

Sae swallowed.

When Taiki and Clint still had not returned by lunchtime, she drove out to Ushidake on a hunch. There she saw Taiki's car parked near the trailhead. Something had happened on the mountain.

Sae called the police. It was nearly five o'clock by the time the Toyama Police Mountain Rescue Squad found Taiki's body at the base of the cliff.

The rescue team with the stretcher reached Sae.

"I think there's no doubt this is your husband, from the driver's license he was carrying. But to be sure, would you mind having a look at the body?" said Toshikasa, one of the squad members.

Taiki's body lay on the stretcher, covered by a sheet.

"Do you think it's better that I don't look at him?" Sae

asked. Taiki himself had told her in gory detail the mess that rocks could make of a body that had fallen from a cliff.

"You could just look at the face. Although it's pretty roughed up."

"All right."

Toshikasa pulled back a corner of the sheet.

"It's my husband," she said reflexively. Sae closed her eyes.

"Thank you. My condolences to you." He replaced the sheet.

Sae turned toward Taiki, put her hands together, and bowed her head.

"We'll take the body to the police station."

"Excuse me, but—" Sae stopped the man.

"What is it?"

"Did you happen to see a dog near where my husband fell? A shepherd crossbreed. They were on the mountain together."

"Apparently the rescue team did spot a dog matching that description. He was on the scree slope where your husband fell, staring down at the body. He ran off when he saw the team. They guessed he belonged to your husband and split up to search for him, but they couldn't find him."

"I see." Sae heaved a sigh. Clint was okay. She felt relieved just to know.

"What's the dog's name? If we call it by name, it might show up."

"It's Clint—no, Tomba," Sae replied.

Since Taiki would have been calling him Tomba the whole time they were on the mountain, Sae had a feeling he'd be more likely to respond to Tomba.

"I'll let the searchers know."

"Thank you." Sae bowed her head again.

The team pushed the stretcher in the direction of the parking lot.

Guilt burned in Sae's breast. *Taiki died because of what I was thinking,* she thought. She had wept upon being informed that a body had been found; now her face was dry.

"I didn't want him to die." She turned her face to the heavens. "Clint, come home. Quickly, please," she prayed to the darkening sky.

"SO YOU NEVER FOUND the dog?" Sumi asked Sae, turning to her after placing a stick of incense on Taiki's altar.

Taiki's body had not been returned to the house until a week after he died. A mandatory autopsy had been conducted, since his death was declared accidental. The funeral had been held two days earlier. Ten days had passed since Clint disappeared.

"It must be hard losing the dog as well as your husband."

"Yes, it's lonely here." Sae smiled faintly.

"What an ungrateful dog."

"Oh, but I don't think so," Sae said.

"And why not?"

"We were a pack. But the pack fell apart. That's why Clint cleared out. He went to find his real pack."

"I don't know what you're going on about, Sae, dear. Do you feel all right?"

"I'm fine, really. By the way, I decided I'd like to take over your field next year."

"Are you sure?"

"Yes. I plan to keep myself busy."

Sae poured tea into a cup. She handed it to Sumi, who took a loud sip.

Yes, Sae had to keep working. She had to keep herself busy from morning to night, so there would be no room for the guilt that tormented her. Before anything else, however, she would get another dog and form a new pack of her own. Sae took another sip of tea.

"Come to think of it, I know somebody who's looking for a home for a pup. What do you think, Sae?" Sumi asked. As if she could read Sae's mind.

Sae's reply came instantly: "Yes, please."

iv

The Prostitute
and the Dog

1

Miwa opened the car window. A bitter December wind blew in, filling the car with cold, dusty air. It failed to cool the heat radiating from her body. Sweat trickled down into her eyes. She wiped it away with her hand, leaving a gritty trail across her forehead.

"I can't stand this." There were traces of black dirt under her fancy acrylic nails that careful cleaning with wet tissues hadn't removed. Miwa wanted to get home as quickly as possible and take a long soak in a hot bath. She wanted to cleanse herself of the grime ground into her skin.

She took a cigarette from the pack in the glovebox and put it to her lips. Her hand trembled as she tried to light it. The tremor would not stop. She gave up and tossed the unlit cigarette out the window.

Suddenly she caught sight of something in the headlights. She slammed on the brakes, sending up a thick cloud of dirt. She rushed to close the window.

"Huh?" Her eyes searched the area around the car. It was possible there were deer out here, or wild boar, but surely not bears?

The dirt settled. There was no sign of any animal in the pool of light from the headlights. Had she imagined it?

Miwa released the breath she had been holding and wiped the sweat from her forehead again. The grittiness got worse. Her hands still shook.

"Dammit." She was just about to pull away when she noticed an animal lying in the road about ten yards ahead. It looked canine, but too big to be a fox or a raccoon dog.

"Don't tell me it's a bear cub." Miwa blinked repeatedly. She remembered what her grandfather always used to say: *Don't get near a bear cub—the mother is bound to be nearby.*

The creature lying in the road didn't look like a bear. She gave a timid blast on the car horn. Night swallowed up the noise. She was in the middle of a forest, where the headlights of her car were the sole source of artificial light.

The thing lifted its head, and she saw its eyes glitter in the headlights. It was a dog. A stray maybe, or wild.

"Outta my way, dog." She honked the horn again. The dog did not move. Its head was raised, and it was wagging its tail.

"I said move, dog. You'll get run over," she shouted, leaning on the horn once more.

Still the dog did not move.

"Come on."

Why do these things always have to happen to me? she thought. Tears pricked her eyes, though a few hours earlier she had sworn never to cry again.

"Get the fuck outta my way!" she yelled, opening the door. She had meant to slam it shut again as soon as the dog moved, but it didn't. It simply kept staring at the car with its head raised, slowly wagging its tail. As if signaling for help.

Miwa got out, went to the back of the car, and opened the trunk. She took out a muddy shovel.

"You want help? You're not gonna jump me, are you? I got a shovel here. Try anything and you'll get it to your face."

Gripping the shovel with both hands, she cautiously approached the dog. It looked like a small German shepherd. Probably a mix of some kind.

"What's the matter?"

The dog wagged its tail even harder when she spoke. It must have been used to people.

"You hurt?"

The dog's flanks appeared to be wet and sticky.

"Is that blood?"

Forgetting her fear, Miwa drew closer to the dog. Its breathing was rough.

"I'm just gonna touch you, okay? Don't bite."

She reached out slowly, so as not to startle the dog, and felt its back leg. When she brought her wet finger up to her eyes, she saw blood.

"You're hurt. What am I going to do?"

She reached inside her jacket for her phone, then stopped short. How could she explain why she was in such a desolate spot at this time of night? Miwa couldn't think of a convincing lie.

"Hang on," she said to the dog, then went back to her car.

She put the shovel away and pulled out a large piece of plastic blue sheeting that she had brought just in case. This was not what she'd had in mind for it, though. She spread the sheeting over the back seat. Then she went back to the dog.

"Ready? I'm going to pick you up."

The dog's blood would get on her clothes, but Miwa didn't care. Her jacket was already covered in mud. She picked up the dog. It was pathetically thin and weighed so little.

"We'll get you to a vet," she told it. She peered into the dog's eyes, and it licked the end of her nose.

THE DOG TURNED OUT to have a cut on its left thigh. The vet at the emergency clinic suggested it might have been from the tusk of a wild boar. He said he would suture it and run some tests. Meanwhile, Miwa went home to clean up. After showering and grabbing a bite to eat, she returned to the clinic.

Miwa wasn't the dog's owner. She could have just left it there. It was enough that she'd taken it in for treatment. But finding the dog in that place, at that time, on that particular day, somehow gave her pause. Not to mention the dog's eyes. Even while badly injured and seeking help, its eyes remained calm. Miwa was curious about that look.

At the reception desk, she was told that the operation had been completed and the dog's life was in no danger. She was relieved to hear it. The veterinary surgeon came to speak with her.

"Ms. Suga, as I suspected, it appears to be a boar injury. You mentioned the dog doesn't belong to you, is that right?"

"Yes. I found it lying in the road."

"In the mountains?"

"Yes."

"He's microchipped. According to the database, the owner lives in Iwate Prefecture. The dog is a four-year-old male, and his name is Tamon. I'll contact the owner tomorrow."

"He's an awfully long way from Iwate. How's he doing?"

The vet smothered a yawn. It was almost dawn. A time when it was natural for most people to feel drowsy, but not Miwa.

"The thigh wound wasn't as bad as it looked. Blood tests show no indication of infectious diseases or other illnesses. But he's very thin. On the verge of malnutrition, I'd say. I could give him a drip of an intravenous nutrition supplement. A couple of days in here and I expect he'll be good as new."

"What'll happen if you don't find the owner?" Miwa asked.

A cloud passed over the vet's face.

"Public Health will take him. They'll try to find a new owner, but if they don't . . ."

"He'll be put down?"

"If you don't want that, perhaps you could take him yourself."

"Me?" Miwa pointed at herself.

"My guess is he's some kind of German shepherd crossbreed, so the chances of anyone coming forward to claim him are very low. If he were a popular or native Japanese breed, it'd be a different story."

Miwa looked down. She had thought she might make time to visit the dog while it was recovering, but that was all. Keeping it was another matter.

"There's no need to decide right away. The owner might take him back. He's still sleeping off the anesthetic, but do you want to take a look at him?"

Miwa nodded before she could think.

"Come this way, please."

She was shown to a room with a plate on the door that read TREATMENT ROOM.

On the other side of the examination table, to the rear, a

number of cages were stacked on top of one another. The dog lay in one of them. He had an intravenous tube attached to his front left leg.

"He doesn't have much strength left, so I expect he'll sleep till morning, even once the anesthetic wears off."

Miwa brought her face up to the cage and peered in. His matted fur was now clean; he must have been bathed. Even asleep, the dog looked self-assured.

"Did you have a fight with a boar?" she whispered.

"Luckily the cut was shallow. We sometimes see hunting dogs in here with tusk wounds a lot worse than this."

"Is he a hunting dog?"

"I doubt it." The vet smiled. "The nurse will call you in ten minutes. Feel free to stay with him till then." The vet disappeared.

Miwa continued to stare at the dog. "What were you doing up that mountain? Why did you get in a fight with a boar all on your own?" she asked the unconscious dog. "Where's your owner? What were you doing coming all the way here from Iwate?" She couldn't help asking, though she knew there would be no response. The questions kept popping into her head.

"Don't worry. If we can't find your owner, you can come home with me."

Miwa turned away from the dog and left the treatment room. She went directly to the reception desk.

"What do I have to do to keep that dog?"

The middle-aged woman behind the desk widened her eyes in surprise.

2

'm home," Miwa called as she opened the front door.

Leo was on the other side, waiting for her. She knew even before she opened the door that he would be there.

He had increased in size and weight since leaving the clinic, and his fur had become glossy from daily brushing. Two weeks had passed since she brought him home. In the end the owner could not be found, so Miwa took him in. Leo slipped easily into a new life with her, never barking unnecessarily or making a mess inside. The two-bedroom condominium had felt too big for one. But with Leo now living there, it felt just right. There was enough space for him to walk around as he pleased whenever Miwa was out.

She hesitated to call him Tamon in case it was a sad reminder of his previous owner. Leo was the name she chose instead, because he reminded her of the white lion in a cartoon she had seen a long time ago.

Miwa offered her hand to Leo, who sniffed it first, then

gently licked the back of it. She let Leo lick her as much as he liked. It felt as if he purified her of the touch of strange men.

"Okay now?"

Once Leo was satisfied, Miwa took off her shoes. First she went to the bathroom and scrupulously washed her hands. Then she put dog food in a bowl and set it down on the edge of the kitchen floor. Leo sat in front of the bowl and looked up at her.

"Okay."

When Miwa gave the word, Leo lifted his haunches and thrust his face into the bowl. Miwa sat at the dining table, watching over him as he ate. The bowl emptied quickly.

"Rest time now," Miwa said to Leo after washing the bowl. She headed to the bathroom for a long shower. The better part of an hour passed before she came out again.

When she had taken Leo home from the clinic, the vet had given Miwa some basic tips about keeping a dog. No walks immediately after meals was one thing he'd told her. Dog food expands in the animal's stomach, and vigorous exercise after a meal can increase the chances of gastric problems.

"Is your stomach settled now? Shall we go for a walk?"

Leo was waiting outside the bathroom door. He knew it was walk time after Miwa had had her shower.

"You're a smart boy, Leo."

Miwa attached his collar and leash, then put her sneakers on.

"Shall we go somewhere different today?"

They left the building and headed for the parking lot. When Leo saw her car, he gave a faint growl. He wasn't being aggressive when he did this, Miwa had recently come to understand—he was excited.

She let Leo in the back seat and started the car. At this early hour, there was very little traffic or activity on the streets of Otsu.

Miwa drove fast, over the speed limit. She liked cars. She liked driving them, or even just sitting in them. The compact car she drove felt like her own mobile private room. When she was inside her car with the doors locked, nobody could mess with her.

When she could find the time, long drives were Miwa's only pleasure.

"Now that I have you, it's easier to unwind," she said to Leo in the back seat. Leo was staring at a fixed point. At that moment it happened to be the same direction the car was heading: west. But if she went north, he faced left, and if she headed south, he turned right. Whenever she went east, he turned to look directly behind him. What was he looking for?

"Let's go to the eastern shore of Lake Biwa. Nobody'll be there at this hour, especially not at this time of year. We can have it all to ourselves."

Leo kept staring in the same direction.

The stoplights at the intersection turned red. Miwa braked.

A blue Suzuki Hustler came toward them from the oncoming lane.

"Must get another car," she muttered, eyeing the Hustler. She had bought her car new a year earlier. It had only three thousand miles or so on it, but she was itching to get rid of it.

The lights switched to green. Miwa pressed her foot on the gas pedal, and the engine roared to life.

"Hmmm, a Hustler . . . I'm sick of small cars. What should I get next?"

Though Miwa liked cars, she wasn't particular about the make. As long as she got good gas mileage, anything was fine with her. Next time she saw Nanae she'd ask her opinion. Nanae did the same kind of work as Miwa to fund her car-customizing habit. She was so much of a car fanatic that she went to the Suzuka Circuit racetrack once a month.

The road came up against Lake Biwa and swung north. Leo faced left, his head pressed against the window. Miwa drove north for a while, until the yacht marina came into view. At the next intersection she turned right, then left at a T-junction, arriving at her destination. A park next to a swimming beach. In the summer it was crowded with vacationers, but when the season ended almost nobody went there.

Every time the car changed direction, Leo turned with it.

"Are you looking for something?" Miwa asked, not expecting an answer, of course. She sighed and switched on the stereo. One of Haruya's favorite songs blared out. She tried skipping a song and shuffling. More of Haruya's music.

"Dammit." Miwa pursed her lips and switched off the stereo. She opened the window. A gust of biting-cold wind blew in.

"Oh, that feels good," she exclaimed.

Leo's face in the rearview mirror swiveled toward Miwa.

"Doesn't it feel good to you too? Dogs like the cold, don't they?"

She raised her voice so it would not be drowned out by the wind. Leo wagged his tail in reply.

"Hey, Leo, how about a song from you," she said, and did an imitation howl. Leo cocked his head to one side.

"No good? Don't I sound like a dog?" Miwa laughed at the sight of Leo's confused face.

Then, all of a sudden, he howled. A real canine howl. Miwa stopped laughing and listened. The howl was long, drawn-out, and powerful, with an undertone of sadness.

"Are you calling out to somebody? Your own kind? Your owner?" Miwa asked.

Leo howled again.

"I'M SUCH AN IDIOT," Miwa mumbled, staring vacantly at the lake. The clear water sparkled under the sunlight pouring down from the eastern sky.

Leo was panting at her feet, his tongue lolling out. He had been frolicking around on the beach to his heart's content.

"The sun rises in the east, doesn't it? If I wanted to see the sun rise over the lake, I'd have to go to Kosei, on the other side."

The eastern shore of Lake Biwa was perfect for viewing sunsets, but its sunrises were unremarkable.

"That wasn't very smart of me. I've always been like this, a bit dumb."

Miwa squatted down to stroke Leo on the head.

"Looks like your leg's all healed."

She felt his back leg where the injury had been. He didn't limp anymore, and fur had grown back in the area that had been shaved.

"You know, you really gave me a scare when I found you," Miwa said. She laughed. "But you know what? You're like me in some ways. Sure, you're smart, but you were waiting on that road for somebody to come along after you got hurt in the mountains."

She turned her face to Leo's, and he licked the tip of her nose.

"The thing is, this time of year, nobody goes down that road at night. Lucky for you I came along. Or did you know I was coming? You hiding something from me?"

There were no sidetracks off that road. It came to a dead

end halfway up the mountain. Any car that went up it would have to go back the same way.

"No, no way." Miwa shook her head and began stroking Leo's back.

The phone in the pocket of her down jacket begin to ring. She removed her glove, exposing the slightly damp back of her hand to the wind. She felt her hand rapidly being robbed of warmth. Though it was a warm winter, it was winter nonetheless. The days were mild, but mornings and nights were bitterly cold.

She pulled her phone from her pocket. It was Kimura, Haruya's bosom buddy. He had fine features and good looks that attracted women. But he was evil. Miwa put away her phone without answering it.

"Brrr, it's cold." She stood up while brushing sand from the hems of her pants. "Let's get back to the car."

Leo submitted to having his leash attached. He never whined or protested that he wanted to play more. He was always docile and obedient. Miwa had read up online about how to train a dog, but it really wasn't necessary with Leo. Almost disappointingly so.

She climbed into the back seat with him. Opening the bottle of mineral water she'd bought at a convenience store along the way, she tipped water into Leo's dish. He quickly drained it dry. Miwa took a sip from the bottle.

"Let's sleep," she said. She stretched along the seat, and Leo climbed on her stomach. Pleasure at the warmth of his body won out over his heaviness. Miwa didn't feel like going home, in case Kimura came around and forced his way in. It had been two weeks since Haruya had disappeared. And Haruya owed Kimura money.

Out here, in the car, nobody could bother her.

Miwa closed her eyes. She didn't feel cold, thanks to the rays of morning sun slanting through the windshield and the warmth from Leo's body.

3

Miwa exited the love hotel and headed for the coin parking lot where she had left her car. The "date club" she contracted with didn't provide someone to escort women to jobs. Instead, women would get a text message telling them which love hotel to go to. Then they would go by themselves, take the fee, and get themselves home. They took out their cut of the money and handed over the rest to a collector at a later date.

Miwa sometimes thought about running off with the money, but when she heard what the consequences were for women who had actually done that, she realized it was not worth the risk.

Men who wanted quick service went to the nearby Ogoto red-light district. Those who didn't care for brothels called Miwa's date club instead. At the most she had three clients a night. The earnings were collected once a week so that not much could be done with the money in between.

Miwa picked up her phone. It was after midnight, and she wanted to finish for the day. Clients were thin on the ground anyway. Everybody was busy at the end of the year, and nobody had money to spare.

The coin parking lot came into view, and Miwa went to take her purse from her handbag. Her feet stopped in their tracks. Someone was leaning on the hood of her car.

She shifted her grip on her phone. Even though the job did not provide escorts, there was always help on standby if a situation arose. Any trouble with a client, and they would come running with one phone call.

Miwa screwed up her eyes. In the dim light of the streetlamp, she couldn't make out who it was. But the silhouette was a man's, and he was smoking a cigarette.

"Yo, Miwa, long time no see." The man turned toward her.

She recognized him. It was Kimura. Miwa stifled a sigh. "What do you want?" she responded bluntly.

"You don't answer your phone, like, so I took the trouble to come and find you."

Kimura threw his cigarette on the ground and crushed it under his heel.

"I'm busy at night, and I sleep during the day."

As Miwa got closer, she could see Kimura's expression more

clearly. The usual sleazy smile was pasted across his pretty-boy face.

"I can't get hold of Haruya. Been two weeks now."

"I haven't seen him either, ever since he took off with my hard-earned money. He's probably gone on another gambling spree," Miwa replied.

Haruya was into every type of gambling. The usual pachinko and mahjong, as well as horses, cycling, and powerboat racing. Otsu had a boat-racing course, and used to have a cycling track as well, but it was closed now. Horse-racing tracks were only slightly farther afield, in Kyoto and Takarazuka. It was a gamblers' paradise. No wonder there were so many like Haruya.

Haruya went to cycling and horse tracks around the country. It wasn't unusual for him to be away for almost a month at a time. His basic pattern was to go off, have a good time as long as his money lasted, and then come crying back to Miwa when it ran out. And squeeze her for more.

"I've always been able to get a hold of him till now, even when he's away gambling," Kimura said. He pulled out another cigarette.

"Well, there's nothing I can do."

Kimura lit up. "He owes me money."

As Miwa suspected. "Oh, does he?" she replied curtly.

"I need it back. Soon."

"Tell that to Haruya."

"Can't get hold of him, can I. S'why I'm here. You're his woman. You pay it back for him."

"You gotta be kidding. I'm the one with a problem. Haruya stripped me bare. He went off with all the money I made selling my body." Miwa pushed past Kimura.

He grabbed her by the left arm. "Don't run away. I'm not done talking to you."

"If anything happens to me, Ozono will have something to say." Miwa dropped the name of the date club manager, who happened to be an associate of the leader of the Blue Dragon crime syndicate.

"I'm not gonna hurt you. I just wanna talk."

"I don't have any money. Even if I wanted to, I couldn't pay you. There's not much work at the moment. Plus the regulars are going over to younger girls."

Miwa was twenty-four. Still young by conventional standards, but in this world she was middle-aged. Men who paid money for women preferred girls no older than twenty.

"That's what happens when you work in a dump of a town like this. You oughtta go to Kyoto or Osaka. A girl like you'd be in demand there."

"Go tell that to some other woman."

Miwa pushed Kimura's hand away from her and paid the parking lot fee. Kimura didn't stop her.

"Anyway, I want that money. Tell Haruya to call me."

"I can't reach him. He's probably living it up on winnings from the tracks. He'll be back when the money runs out."

"That's why I wanna catch hold of him now, while he still has some."

"Well, there's nothing I can do."

Miwa got in her car. She shut the door and started the engine. Kimura was still standing there, puffing on his cigarette and fixing Miwa with a hard stare.

"How about trading Haruya in for me? I'll show you a good time," he said.

"Fuck off," Miwa spat out. She shoved the gearstick into drive.

Kimura flicked away his cigarette. It hit the windshield, sending out a shower of sparks.

Miwa pulled away roughly. Kimura made a big show of jumping out of her way. The smirk on his face infuriated her. Her nerves were already on edge after tonight's client, a brute who had demanded kinky stuff. Now thanks to Kimura she was even more wound up.

The stoplights at the intersection just before the main avenue turned red. Miwa put her foot on the brake and came to a stop. She closed her eyes, her foot still on the pedal. She thought of Leo's face. *Help me, Leo. Make me pure again.* She prayed to the image of Leo in her head, looking at her with eyes that could see into her heart.

MIWA WAS ON HER guard as she approached the condo block. She couldn't be sure that Kimura hadn't beaten her back there. It would be just like him to do that. He was a tenacious prick. Luckily her fears were not realized. She saw no sign of him and entered the lobby with relief. She took the elevator to the sixth floor and unlocked her door. Ordinarily, Leo would be waiting on the other side, but tonight he wasn't there.

"Leo?" she called as she took off her shoes. But Leo did not show himself. "What's wrong, Leo?"

Anxiously, Miwa flung her bag down and hurried inside. She found Leo lying facedown in the middle of the living room, which was splattered with vomit.

"Leo, what's wrong? What happened?"

Ignoring the mess, Miwa lifted Leo up. He lay limp in her arms.

"No. This can't be. Leo, snap out of it."

Leo opened his eyes. He raised his head and licked Miwa's cheek. The lick was feeble, and she could tell he was weak.

"We're going to the vet. Leo, hang in there."

Still holding Leo, Miwa stood up and headed for the front

door. She left without even locking up. The elevator ride felt like an eternity. Back in the parking lot again, she ran to the car and lay Leo down in the back seat.

"How can this be happening?"

Miwa sped off. She headed for the same veterinary hospital where she had taken Leo the night she found him. She knew it had an emergency night clinic. On the way, she called to notify the clinic she was coming. The staff promised to be ready to examine Leo the minute she arrived.

"Hang in there, Leo. Don't die on me." Her chest felt tight with worry and fear. Though Leo had been with her only a short time, he was irreplaceable. Miwa couldn't imagine life without him.

She reached the hospital in ten minutes flat. During the day, the trip would easily have taken a half hour. Good thing she hadn't been stopped for speeding. A vet and nurse were waiting, as promised. They brought a stretcher out to the parking lot and carried Leo into the treatment room. Miwa filled in the vet as they walked.

"He appears to be having trouble breathing but he isn't vomiting now," the vet said after taking Leo's pulse. "We'll do a blood test first. Then, depending on the results, an X-ray or maybe even an MRI."

"Do whatever you have to," Miwa implored. She continued to

pray in the waiting room. *Please, god, save Leo. Don't take him from me.* She could not remember ever praying before. She didn't even believe in any gods in the first place. But now she was prepared to throw herself at their mercy, even though she didn't believe.

The vet emerged from the treatment room. Miwa rose from the sofa and hurried over to him. He held a piece of paper in his hands. "He has acute kidney failure."

The words were a knife in Miwa's heart.

He showed her the paper with the results of the blood test and said something about urea. But his words went in one ear and out the other. All she could think was *Kidney failure? That's bad*, over and over.

"Ms. Suga?" The vet had to say her name several times before Miwa snapped back to reality.

"Oh . . . yes."

"Has he been drinking more than usual?"

Miwa nodded. Come to think of it, the past few days Leo had been drinking probably twice as much water as he usually did.

"We can't tell the cause from a blood test alone, but my guess is it's most likely due to a virus."

"A virus?"

"I believe you found the dog in the mountains, no? Which means it's possible a tick bit him. It's common for symptoms to appear sometime after transmission occurs. The kidneys become strained fighting the infection and unable to perform their normal function of expelling urine."

"Will he recover?" Miwa asked. She wanted to throw herself at the vet's feet and plead with him to do everything in his power to save Leo.

"Since it's acute, not chronic, he ought to recover in a week if we give him steroids to lower immunity and expel the toxic waste. We can keep him for a day of observation, to be on the safe side."

"A week?" Miwa couldn't believe her ears.

"Yes. Judging by his recovery from the previous injury, this boy is basically strong and healthy. So my guess is a week, maybe even less."

"Thank you so much."

"I doubt it'll be necessary, but once he recovers we could do another blood test in a week's time if you're worried."

"Yes. Thank you. Thank you so much."

The vet smiled.

"Ms. Suga, I think this is the first dog you've had? It must have been quite a shock when you found him limp and vomiting. But your bringing him in for treatment so quickly prevented this from becoming too serious. All I can do is examine him and give him drugs."

"Even so, thank you very much."

Miwa bowed her head deeply.

BACK IN HER APARTMENT, Miwa felt fatigue come crashing down on her. The sky was growing light. She took a shower, poured herself a glass of white wine, and sat sipping it.

Leo was not there. Without him, her place felt enormous. Lonely and sad. She poured herself another glass of wine to chase away the loneliness.

Ms. Suga, I think this is the first dog you've had? The vet's words rang in her ears. She had never owned a dog herself, but she remembered her grandfather's dog very well.

Her grandfather had been a farmer and hunter who lived in a wooded area close to the border between Shiga and Fukui Prefectures. He had lived alone ever since her grandmother passed away when she was only in her fifties. Being a professional hunter, he always had a hunting dog.

Miwa's dad was the second son in the Suga family. He went to Nagoya University and settled down in Otsu to be close enough to keep an eye on his father. His older brother, the elder son, went to Tokyo to work, and his sister moved to Osaka when she married. Miwa's dad had thought somebody should be a reasonable distance from his father, yet he himself was always buried in work. He saw him only a few times a year, during the summer Obon festival, for the New Year, and over the holiday week in May.

Miwa's grandfather was a difficult man, not good at talking to people. Miwa was terrified of him. He rarely ever smiled or spoke to her. But his expression would change whenever he spoke to his dog, Yamato. Yamato was a Kishu, a breed native to Japan. As a little girl, Miwa was convinced Yamato possessed magical powers. She saw how Yamato had the ability to turn her scary grandfather into a smiling, less intimidating person. Whenever they went to her grandfather's house, Miwa always stuck close to the dog so she could see her grandfather smile. Besides, touching Yamato made her feel warm. Yamato in turn was gentle with her.

Miwa was eight when Yamato died. She cried the whole night through for Yamato, and for her grandfather. When Yamato died, her grandfather stopped hunting. Age had probably caught up with him.

How long had it been since she'd thought about them? There had been no dogs in Miwa's life ever since.

She took another sip of wine. "I wish I could see him again. And Yamato," she said.

Leo reminded her of Yamato. He melted her heart the same way Yamato had her grandfather's. He had the power to make her smile.

"It's lonely without you, Leo." Miwa placed her glass on the table. She crawled over to her bed and under the covers. Leo usually warmed them for her, but tonight they were cold.

eo, not that way," Miwa scolded when he tried to veer off their usual route. Obediently, Leo resumed walking by her side.

Miwa stifled a sigh. Recently, Leo was trying more and more often to go his own way down some alley or other. If they were heading north, he wanted to go left. If they were going south, he would try to turn right. It was the same in the car too. Leo, it seemed, wanted to go west. Miwa was sure of it. She was certain he had been on his way west through the mountains when he'd gotten into a fight with a wild boar.

Who was in the west? The owner he'd been separated from? She found that hard to believe. Leo's owner was in Iwate, way up north. Miwa tried to deny the possibility to herself, but with Leo anything was possible. Maybe the owner had moved away from Iwate.

She remembered seeing a report on TV about a dog reunited

with its owner after traveling a few hundred—or was it a few thousand—miles. Maybe dogs had powers that humans simply didn't have the capacity to fathom.

"Are you looking for your owner? Is that it?" Miwa said to Leo. He heard her, of course, but did not react. He simply kept walking at the same pace as Miwa.

"Don't you like being with me? Aren't you happy?"

Leo stopped. Slowly, he turned his face up to hers. His thoughtful eyes looked her over. She looked back into them. Leo's jet-black eyes were so deep she could have drowned in them, but she found no answer to her questions there.

"Sorry. That was out of line." Miwa started walking again.

Leo had completely recovered thanks to the vet's treatment. The results from his follow-up blood tests were all clear, and the vet had pronounced a relapse unlikely.

Once Leo had recovered, Miwa resumed their dawn walks. After arriving home from work, she would feed Leo and take a shower. Then they would go out. She liked the feel of the winter air on her skin, still fresh from the shower, and their walks had unintentionally grown longer each day.

Thanks to this daily exercise, Miwa's health improved. Before meeting Leo, Miwa had been unable to sleep without first drowning herself in alcohol to erase the smell of men that clung to her body. Now when she came home, Leo licked her hand. It made her feel less dirty somehow. Purified. And she drank less.

They came to a major road and turned right, then walked for a while along the wide sidewalk. The next intersection was where they usually turned right again, onto a small shopping street. They would cut across it and go down a narrow street between the houses. But today there was a car driving along the main road that did a U-turn and came back toward them. A Honda sports car with a customized suspension and a loudly tuned engine.

As the car pulled up alongside Miwa and Leo, the passenger window rolled down. Kimura showed his face.

"Hey, since when've you had a dog?"

"Since recently," Miwa snapped back.

"I thought Haruya hated animals? Shit'll hit the fan when he gets back."

"He had no choice. I told him I'd quit work if he didn't let me have a dog."

Kimura smirked at the lie. "He'll have to suck it up, then. So, when'd you two talk?"

"Before he went away."

"A whole month ago."

"Probably winning for a change. He won't be back while the money lasts."

"He'll come running back as soon as the money runs out. That guy's crap at gambling—no way he can keep on winning for a month."

"Maybe it's a once-in-a-lifetime streak. Come on, let's go," Miwa said to Leo, and walked off.

"Y'know, Miwa, there are rumors. People say you did away with Haruya."

Miwa stopped in her tracks.

"You told one of the girls at the date club that you wanted to kill him, didn't you? Haruya's scum, for sure. It wouldn't be any wonder if you did get rid of him. That's what some people are saying."

Miwa turned around. "Saying I'd like to kill him and actually doing it are not the same." Her heart thumped wildly.

Leo bared his fangs and growled.

"That night in the parking lot. While I was waiting for you, I checked out the inside of your car. Through the window, like, just to kill time. There was blue plastic sheeting in the back. With stains on it—Haruya's blood, I'm guessing."

It was all Miwa could do to stop the shaking. Kimura was trying to trip her up. She knew it—she couldn't fall into his trap.

If only she'd gotten rid of that blue sheeting. But with all the business with Leo, and looking after him, she'd ended up leaving it in the car.

"How about I pay the cops a visit? Tell them my friend Haruya Moriguchi has been missing for a month. Whaddaya think about that, Miwa?"

"Go to hell."

"Pay back the five hundred thousand yen he owes me, and I'll forget about the blue sheeting."

"There's nothing to forget."

"If I tell the police you buried him in the mountains, they'll soon find the body."

Miwa shook her head. She was distracted by Leo, tugging on his leash and growling.

"You've got till the day after tomorrow. Five hundred thou. Got that?"

Kimura's face disappeared. His car rumbled loudly. Leo barked. The car raced off, leaving behind a cloud of exhaust.

"Leo, stop it."

Leo kept barking.

"I said stop."

Miwa yanked roughly on the leash. Leo stopped. He looked up at her, bewildered. *Why did you stop me when I was only trying to protect you?* his eyes seemed to say.

"I'm sorry." Miwa squatted down and hugged him.

A dam inside her broke. Everything she'd held back while talking to Kimura surged to the surface. She couldn't stop shaking.

"What do I do, Leo? What am I going to do?"

Leo wagged his tail and licked Miwa's cheeks.

The thought of his trying to comfort her made Miwa's eyes spill over with tears. "Thank you, my friend. I love you."

Thanks to Leo's warmth, Miwa stopped trembling. His kindness tugged at her heart. "It's your dog magic, I suppose. Dogs don't just make people smile. They give us love and courage, too, just from being at our side."

She remembered her grandfather, who would have received the same kind of love and courage from his dog, Yamato. With Yamato there, it didn't bother him to be living on his own in a tiny village deep in the mountains. But after Yamato died, her grandfather had visibly declined. When Miwa's father suggested he get another dog, he flat-out refused.

What'll happen to the dog when I die? Are you gonna take care of it? he'd demanded. Her father had gone quiet at that. Even if he'd wanted a dog, Miwa's mother would never have agreed. Her mother did not like animals. And with her father out of the house most of the time for work, any dog they took in would have to be cared for by her mother.

Five years after Yamato's death, Miwa's grandfather collapsed at home. A deliveryman found him. By the time he was taken to the hospital, he was already dead.

If he had gotten another dog after Yamato died, what would have happened to it? A chill ran down Miwa's back.

"What would happen to you if I disappeared, Leo?" She pulled away from him to look him in the eyes.

Leo returned her gaze squarely.

MIWA'S BOSS, Yanagida, scowled when she asked him for an advance. Eventually he handed her five bundles of 100,000 yen each—more than twice her monthly earnings—after she swore to work her butt off to repay it.

"I'm not charging interest, 'cause you're an employee. But if I don't get it back, you can go work in Ogoto."

At a brothel, in other words. Miwa nodded as she put the money in her bag.

Just then, she got a text message. One of her regular clients wanted her. Miwa left the office and headed for the love hotel where the client was waiting. This man was a good customer. He paid well, never asked for anything unreasonable, and sometimes tipped extra when he could spare it. He also usually told Miwa to skip the blow job, because of his tendency to ejaculate prematurely.

This was the kind of client Miwa liked. If selling your body was what you had to do, then many girls in the business preferred hand jobs or blow jobs as the better part of the deal, but not Miwa. For her, relief at not having to do extras outweighed her distaste for penetration. Getting fucked was the basic trans-

action. Anything else on top of that was merely more unpleas-
antness that she preferred to avoid.

She knocked on the door. The client beckoned her in. She
took a shower, then lay down on the bed with a towel wrapped
around her. The man leaned over her, opened up the towel,
and began to feel her breasts and crotch. Miwa reached for his
penis. It was already stiff.

While gently stroking the man's penis, Miwa closed her eyes.
Her mind went to another place. *Keep mind and body apart.* That
was how she dealt with this brutal reality. The problem was,
she couldn't always control where her mind went. Sometimes
it returned to an incident just an hour earlier; other times it
went back to her childhood.

Today, her mind went back to *that day*.

A friend of Haruya's had called her: Was it true he'd won
big on the horses? If so, then this person wanted his loan back.
That was the gist of the call. Miwa hung up without saying
anything, then contacted one of Haruya's horse-racing buddies.

Had Haruya really had a big win? He had. Apparently a few
days earlier at the Hanshin Racecourse, he'd spent 1,000 yen
on a trifecta ticket with nearly 100,000 yen on it. The return
was roughly 1,000,000 yen.

Miwa had seen Haruya the day before. He'd been in a good
mood, so she'd assumed he must have had a win, probably a

small one. But pocketing almost 1,000,000 yen . . . not in a million years would she have imagined that.

If I win on the horses, I'll pay you back. That was probably the line he'd used on the caller.

Miwa had originally gone into the adult entertainment business to help Haruya repay his gambling debts after he'd come crying to her. But he took the money she earned and used it to get in even deeper. As Haruya's debts mounted, Miwa kept changing jobs, going from one business to another that offered various sexual services, until eventually she reached outright prostitution.

All that, and he hadn't told her about his win.

It wasn't that she wanted him to give the million yen to her. It just might have been nice if he'd used it to show her some sign of appreciation. Take her on a trip, maybe, or out for a nice meal.

Blinding rage consumed her. If she stayed inside the apartment a minute longer, Miwa felt she would explode. So she got into her car and went driving, aimlessly. After going once around Lake Biwa, she came back to Otsu. By then it was dark. She phoned the date club to say she wasn't feeling well and couldn't come in that night.

It was then that she spotted Haruya, while at the lights of a large intersection near the city center. She saw him through the window of a steak house. He had a mouth full of food and a glass of red wine in his hand. In the seat opposite him was a stranger, a young woman.

Steak, with red wine? When he's never even taken me out for cheap barbecue?

To Haruya, Miwa was nothing more than someone who gave him money and sex whenever he wanted. That was the bottom line. And that was who she'd sold her body for.

This ends now. Miwa had had enough of being used by Haruya.

She went to a home improvement store and bought a knife, a rope, blue plastic sheeting, and a shovel. At another store she purchased an oversize suitcase. It wasn't like she had a specific plan. She was just doing what needed to be done.

Haruya came home the next morning. When Miwa asked where he'd been the night before, he coolly lied and said he'd been playing mahjong.

I took a bit of a hit, Miwa. Sorry, but can you lend me some more money?

The instant she heard this, Miwa's mind was made up.

Picking up the knife, she casually approached Haruya from behind. Then she stabbed him, repeatedly. When he'd stopped moving, she cut off his clothes, tore them into pieces, and stuffed them into a garbage bag. She struggled to drag him into the bathroom and then watched his blood disappear down the drain. When the flow of blood stopped, she returned to the living room and painstakingly scrubbed all the blood from the floor and walls.

Miwa stuffed Haruya's body into the suitcase and then took a shower, at the same time carefully rinsing all traces of blood from the bathroom.

Then she waited for night to fall before hauling the suitcase out to her car. She lined the trunk with the blue sheeting, in case any blood should leak out. And she tossed in the shovel as well as the knife, which she had scrubbed clean of Haruya's blood.

There was a mountain she knew. Near the village where her grandfather used to live. She had once hiked it with her grandfather. At the time he'd said: *If you buried a body here, no one would ever find it.* A forestry road went partway up the mountain, but after that you had to plow through forest and thickets to go any farther. The only people who went to a place like that nowadays were hunters, but there weren't many of those anymore.

She drove cautiously, taking care to obey the speed limit. Her heart skipped a beat every time a car came from the other direction. At one point she spotted a flashing red police light in the distance. It was all up, she thought. But the patrol came no closer. She met with no trouble along the way.

Midway up the mountain, she dug a hole. It was hard work, and she became sweaty and covered in mud. She tossed the suitcase and the knife into the hole, and by the time she had finished filling it in, she was exhausted.

All she wanted was to get home as fast as possible, take a shower, and fall into a deep sleep. When she woke up in the morning, she would leave this city. Haruya had debts everywhere. Once his disappearance became known, his debtors would come knocking on Miwa's door. Everybody knew she was Haruya's woman.

Where should she go? Okinawa would be nice. So would Hokkaido. Miwa gave a mean blow job. She could make a living with her mouth wherever she went. If that didn't work out, she could resort to turning tricks again.

Such were the thoughts running through her head when she'd come across Leo on the mountain road.

Why did it have to be that night and that place? Miwa had often wondered this since finding Leo. But there was no turning back. Leo and Miwa had met because they were meant to.

THE SOUND OF PANTING pulled her back to the present. Miwa opened her eyes and saw the customer writhing his hips over her. In his face she saw Haruya's.

"Ugh!" Instinctively she pushed him off her. He rolled away to the end of the bed, lying on his back with his arms and legs flung out, his condom-sheathed penis sticking straight up.

"What the hell?"

The customer's face twisted with rage. He looked exactly like Haruya used to when he was angry.

Miwa kicked the man in the face. A sharp pain ran up her shin. There was a bottle of whiskey on a table in the corner of the room. She reached for it and brought it down on his head. He covered his face and groaned. Then he fell flat on the floor and didn't move.

Miwa hastily got dressed. She left the hotel, taking care to avoid seeing anyone on her way out. Once she was in her car, she began to splutter and choke. Was he dead? If he wasn't, he was sure to lodge a complaint with the club manager. What a mess, and just when she had borrowed 500,000 yen. The manager would be furious. She was in deep shit.

"I have to get away," Miwa said as she started the car.

What about Leo? another part of her asked. She agonized over what to do. Then an image of her grandfather's face flashed through her mind. *What'll happen to the dog when I die?*

She heard her grandfather's voice: *What will happen to Leo if you go to jail?* She could see her grandfather staring at her. With eyes exactly like Leo's.

Miwa rested her head on the steering wheel and sobbed.

5

As always, Leo faced west. Miwa bit her lip as she steered the car. The phone she'd tossed on the passenger seat buzzed with a text message. It was Kimura. *Of course.* The text was just as predictable: *Where's my money?*

Miwa snorted. "You gonna come and collect it from jail?"

Then she got a phone call. This time it was the club manager. Miwa had checked the news online but found nothing about a death. She had also returned the money she'd borrowed, leaving it in the mailbox at the club office. There was no reason for her to answer the phone just to get her head bitten off.

The road sign informed her that she had left Shiga Prefecture and was now in Kyoto. She could see on her dashboard that she was almost out of gas. Her plan was to go as far west as her car would take her, then look for a police station and turn herself in.

"Before I go to the cops . . ." Miwa muttered.

West, west, Leo wanted to go west. Where, exactly? Miwa

didn't know, but she was going to do her best to take him as far west as she possibly could.

She turned off the national route and followed a road that wound through the mountains. Though still within the Kyoto city precincts, the area was forested. Unlike on the highway, there was little traffic. When she spotted a convenience store, she pulled up to buy dog food and water. Then she continued driving again. The gas gauge started to flash after she had crossed into the Kyotamba district. The road was a narrow one that connected tiny villages dotted through the mountains. Rice and vegetable fields were squeezed into the sparse acreage of valleys in between.

Miwa turned the car down a forest road. The trees on the surrounding mountain slopes were bare. An atmosphere of melancholy hung over the area.

Ten minutes down the road, Miwa stopped the car. She filled Leo's bowl with food, then got out of the car. When she opened the door, Leo bounded out from the back.

"Eat up," Miwa said. "You were just skin and bones when I met you. Not easy catching your own food, is it? Eat up while you can."

The bowl emptied in a flash. She refilled it. This, too, quickly disappeared into Leo's stomach. When he finished eating, Leo looked up at Miwa.

"Had enough? Want some water? Not too much. Your guts'll get all twisted."

She removed the lid and tilted the bottle slightly. Leo deftly licked up the water that trickled out. When the bottle was half empty, Miwa put the lid back on.

"That's all. And now this."

From her pocket she took out a good-luck charm bag with a folded, handwritten note inside.

> *This dog's name is Tamon. I found him in the mountains in Shiga. He was injured in a fight with a wild boar. I think he is heading west to try to find his owner. If you meet Tamon, please help him to travel west. Please, he's a really good dog. You won't be able to help wanting to keep him. But he has his own family. I hope whoever reads this note will feel the same as me and give him all the help you can.*
>
> *May Tamon meet with kindness along the way and find his family again.*
>
> *Miwa*

Miwa threaded the tiny bag through Leo's collar so it wouldn't come off.

"Leo."

When she called his name, Leo pushed against her. He was a smart dog. He knew this was goodbye.

"What is your family like, I wonder? How did you lose them? They must be kind people, considering how much you want to find them again. I wish I had family like that."

Miwa pulled Leo close to her. After taking up with Haruya, she'd become estranged from her own family because she couldn't take her mother's constant bad-mouthing of him. Then when she'd started working in the adult entertainment business, she'd completely cut her ties. She couldn't look her parents or younger brother in the eyes anymore. It hurt to admit that her mother had been right.

How pained would her parents—those kind people—be when they saw her on the TV news. What would her brother think?

She was the one who'd thrown away the comfort of family for Haruya. She was the one who'd given in to Haruya's every word. She was the one who'd killed him. There was no denying that.

She was here because this was the path she'd chosen. No one else was to blame.

"I'm so glad I met you. It was the best thing that ever happened in my whole shitty life. I was truly happy being with you."

Leo licked Miwa's cheek. *I was happy too*, he seemed to say.

"You're such a smart, kind boy. Thank you, Leo. I know you'll find your family. I hope you'll be happy."

Miwa stood up, reluctantly pulling away from the last of Leo's warmth.

Leo looked up at Miwa.

"Off you go now. It's okay."

Leo turned around and ran off. Deep into the forest.

"No more fighting wild boar," Miwa called out as Leo rapidly disappeared. She bit her lip hard, fighting back tears.

The Old Man
and the Dog

1

Yaichi was flicking through the TV channels while sipping from a mug of shochu. He scowled: there was nothing decent on. When he reached NHK, he put down the remote control and sucked on a piece of deer jerky with his shochu while he watched the evening news.

The prime minister's face appeared. One of his cabinet members had made yet another crass blunder. "Blathering idiot," he railed at the figure on the screen, whose home electorate happened to be in the neighboring prefecture.

He poured himself more shochu. But after lifting the mug to his lips, he held it still. There was a noise. Something that didn't come from the TV. He pricked up his ears and heard it again. The sound of dry leaves crunching underfoot.

Yaichi got up and crept to the next room. His gun locker was there, next to the family altar. He turned the key, took out his hunting rifle, and loaded it. Then, sliding his arm through the sling, he hung it from his shoulder.

The footsteps were too light to be those of a bear, and deer moved in herds. In all likelihood it was a boar. Hungry and lost. Luckily, there was a full moon tonight. He wouldn't need a light to shoot by.

Yaichi put on his trekking boots and went out the back door. He could hear the animal still roaming about the garden. He slipped the gun off his shoulder and held it with both hands. He hadn't hunted since losing his hunting dog, Masakado, last spring. But he hadn't lost his touch.

Under the bright autumn moonlight, Yaichi made his way along the outer wall of the house to the front garden. The cold, brittle air mocked him. All remnants of alcohol in his brain evaporated.

He raised the rifle. Both arms to his sides, cheek pressed firmly against the gunstock. This was the decisive moment. He had to bring down his quarry before it noticed him. Yaichi quickened his step. Estimating the animal's position from the sound of its footsteps, he aimed the gun. Then in one fluid movement, he leapt into the garden, ready to squeeze the trigger, but in that instant his fingers froze.

The creature was a dog. Thin and filthy. Yaichi locked eyes with it at the other end of his rifle. He saw the strength and determination in its eyes.

"Oy, you scared the shit outta me." He lowered his gun.

The dog didn't move. It continued to stand stock-still, staring at Yaichi. It looked like it hadn't eaten in days. Despite its half-starved appearance, Yaichi wasn't getting any sense of weakness from it.

Tough dog, Yaichi immediately concluded. He had no doubt that this was one hardy dog, in body and spirit. It was the kind of dog that could lead and protect a pack. Probably an excellent hunting dog, too, if given proper training.

"Here," Yaichi said. The dog walked up to him. It seemed used to humans. *Must be a stray,* he thought.

He went over to the front door and opened it. The dog followed him to the packed-dirt floor of the entrance hall. "Stay," he commanded. The dog stopped. It had understood.

Yaichi crossed the living room into the kitchen. He drew the bolt to eject the round, returned the bolt, then left the rifle on the kitchen table that he hardly ever used. Opening up the industrial-size freezer crammed with the meat of deer and boar that he had killed and butchered himself, he pulled out a pound of deer meat, tossed it into the microwave, and pressed defrost. Then he filled a shallow aluminum Yukihira saucepan with water and brought it back to the dog.

The dog was lying on the dirt floor. As Yaichi approached, it raised its head. It hadn't let down its guard. But it wasn't on high alert, either.

"Drink." Yaichi set the water down in front of it. The dog rose to its feet, thrust its nose into the saucepan, and drank.

"Where in the world did you come from? I nearly shot you. You coulda been killed," Yaichi said.

The dog lifted its ears but didn't stop drinking.

"Ya must be starving. I'll feed you some meat once it thaws."

At the words *feed you*, the dog stopped drinking.

"So ya can tell when there's food on offer. Smart dog," Yaichi said.

The dog started drinking again.

Yaichi observed it. It looked like a mix. A cross of native Japanese and German shepherd. But its torso was longer than a Japanese breed's, and its loins were lower to the ground. Its tail, too, was long. Dried leaves and twigs were tangled in its gray-tinged fur. Though thin, its frame was covered in strong muscle. Yaichi didn't see any sign of a collar.

When the dog had drunk all the water, it lay down again. Yaichi took the saucepan back to the kitchen. The meat hadn't finished defrosting, but he stopped the microwave anyway and removed it. That dog looked capable of handling partially frozen meat. He cut it into pieces, tossed them into the same saucepan, and brought it back to the entrance hall.

The dog was standing. It had caught the scent of meat. Desperate as it was to eat, however, it had obeyed Yaichi's command to stay in the entrance. Yaichi was impressed. "Smart dog," he said, setting down the saucepan at the dog's feet.

The dog did not move. It remained still, staring at Yaichi, waiting. Not like when he had given it the water.

"Go on, eat," he said, and the dog thrust its nose into the saucepan. It crunched noisily on the partially frozen meat.

"Gotta put away the gun," Yaichi muttered, heading to the kitchen table to retrieve it. He carried it to the gun locker. His gun was an M1500 rifle made by Howa Machinery, purchased twenty years ago and kept in perfect working order ever since. He never neglected daily maintenance. Even now that he didn't use it anymore, he still kept up a routine of dismantling, cleaning, and reassembling it, grumbling to himself all the while about what the point was. For more than fifty years he'd made a living from hunting, and it was a lingering attachment to his trade that held him back from turning in his hunter's license and getting rid of the gun. He just couldn't do it. He placed the M1500 back in the locker and turned the key.

By the time Yaichi returned to the entrance hall, the dog had finished eating and was lying with its eyes closed. Asleep. It was completely spent.

Yaichi settled himself down in the living room. He reached for his mug and gazed at the sleeping dog's face as he sipped on his shochu, not once tiring of the sight.

aichi attached Masakado's old leash and collar to the dog, got him onto the back of his mini truck, and set out for town for the first time in a long while.

He pulled up outside Kamata Veterinary Hospital and took the dog inside. Consultation hours hadn't started yet, and the waiting room was empty.

"Well, if it isn't Yaichi," said Seiji Kamata, the vet, showing his face as Yaichi reached the front desk. Yaichi had entrusted Dr. Kamata with the care of successive generations of his hunting dogs for more than thirty years.

"And look at this, did you get yourself another dog? I thought you said you were done hunting when Masakado died."

"It's a stray, Doctor. Turned up in my garden last night."

"Is that so? You don't see many strays these days."

"I brought him in for a checkup and shampoo. He's pretty scrawny and dirty. Looks like he might've been roaming the mountains for quite a while."

"In that case we need to check for infectious diseases and ticks as well."

"While you're at it, could ya take a photo and put it on that internet?"

Dr. Kamata had a page on his hospital website to help find owners and new homes for dogs and cats that had been taken into the shelter. Their photos were posted, along with details of appearance and personality. He'd had a reasonable degree of success in placing animals this way.

"No problem. I'll check to see if he has a microchip as well. Fill out the form, and I'll look him over right away." Dr. Kamata patted the dog on the head a few times, then disappeared into the examining room.

"Mr. Katano, would you fill out this form, please?" the nurse-receptionist said.

Yaichi took the sheet of paper and sat down on the long bench in the waiting room. As he went to fill in the blanks, his hand stopped at the column for the dog's name. He hesitated, then wrote down Noritsune.

Yaichi named his dogs mainly after samurai warriors from the Genji and Heike clans. Masakado was named for Taira no Masakado. Noritsune for Taira no Noritsune. This was the most he could do with the form. He knew nothing about the dog's age or its medical history.

"Sorry, s'all I've got." Yaichi handed it to the receptionist.

"You only know its name?"

"Even that I just made up," Yaichi replied. "Ain't that so, Noritsune? Truth is, you're nameless."

The dog—Noritsune—looked up at Yaichi and slowly wagged his tail.

NORITSUNE WAS THIN, but apart from that Dr. Kamata could find nothing wrong with him. No ticks, which weren't active this time of year anyway. The vet did, however, find a microchip. It revealed that his owner was in Iwate. And that the dog's name was Tamon.

"How did he come to be in Shimane Prefecture?" Dr. Kamata was perplexed.

While Noritsune was being shampooed, Yaichi went shopping. He bought vegetables and shochu at the supermarket—with a freezer full of deer and wild boar meat, he didn't need any protein. Or rice, which he grew himself.

Hatsue, his wife, had worked the rice and vegetable fields by herself when she was alive. Yaichi took over four years ago, when she fell ill. By then, his income from hunting had been dwindling for some years, and thoughts of retirement had already entered his mind, so it was a natural enough transition. But even once Hatsue died, he stuck with the fieldwork. She had devoted her life to this patch of earth. Looking after her fields was his way of honoring her memory.

At the home improvement store, he selected a new leash and collar and loaded a large bag of dry dog food onto his shopping cart. He wheeled it to the cash register.

"Now look at this. Did ya get yourself another dog?" the woman behind the register asked.

"Nope, it's for a stray," he said. Yaichi spoke wryly. He was aware, as the words came out, that if a stray dog was going back to its owner, he didn't need this much food. While watching the woman scan the barcode on the bag of dog food, the thought crystallized—he was going to keep Noritsune.

YAICHI'S FINAL PURCHASE was painkillers at the drugstore. Then he went back to the vet hospital.

Noritsune was freshly washed and standing tall. "You don't like being dirty, do ya? You're not just smart, but proud too," Yaichi said. He attached the newly purchased collar and leash.

"We couldn't reach the owner, so I'll upload his information on the website today," the receptionist informed Yaichi when he finished paying.

"If you wouldn't mind, thank you," Yaichi said. But he felt guilty. He was hoping the owner wouldn't be found.

Hatsue had died three years ago and Masakado just six

months ago. Yaichi had expected he could get along just fine on his own, but it was harder than he'd thought. Noritsune's arrival stirred up memories of better days.

Once back home, Yaichi fed Noritsune some dry food mixed with deer meat, then let him go in the garden. Noritsune might wander off, but he would come back. For some reason Yaichi was sure of it.

Noritsune was exploring the garden, sniffing out corner after corner, when he abruptly lifted his head and pointed in the direction of the woodland at the base of the mountain. His nose twitched, his ears pricked, and his tail stood high. He was a magnificent sight: poised, proud, and full of confidence.

As a small car driving up the slope came into view, he gave a low growl. Yaichi's house was in the woods halfway up the mountain, while his fields were at the bottom.

The car belonged to Isao Tamura. "It's all right, Noritsune," Yaichi said. "He ain't an enemy."

Noritsune relaxed.

Isao's car entered the property and stopped. Noritsune resumed his low growl but gave no sign of moving even after Tamura got out.

"Well, I'll be darned, Yaichi, got yourself another dog?" Isao examined Noritsune while scratching his bald head with one hand.

"He's a stray. I took him in till the owner turns up."

"A stray? In this neck of the woods? Why'd he turn up here when there's all them houses in the village down below?" Isao regarded Noritsune curiously.

"He was probably roaming the mountains. My place was prob'ly closer than anyone else's."

"What's he doing in the mountains—"

"If I knew that, it'd be easy, wouldn't it? But he can't talk. Anyway, whaddaya want?"

"Ah, yeah. You know about the town council elections comin' up next month? Well, I came to ask for your vote for Teppei." Tamura held out a leaflet produced by the Teppei Nakamura Campaign Committee. Nakamura had been a town councilor for nearly twenty years. He had used his sway in the position to become head of the local hunting club and to carve out his own little fiefdom, despite abysmal hunting and rifle skills.

"Get outta here. I ain't voting for him."

"Don't say that, Yaichi. He's one of us, the hunting club."

"I quit the hunting club a long time ago."

"Your name's still on the members roll. Teppei says he couldn't very well let the best hunter in the district go. How's that, huh? So what about it, giving him your vote?"

"Ya know I can't stand the schmuck," Yaichi snarled.

The next moment, Noritsune bared his fangs at Isao and growled. Isao went pale. "Whoa, vicious dog. You never know with a stray if it's trained or not. Keep it chained up, why doncha."

"He's all right. A hundred times smarter than any of your idiot dogs," Yaichi jeered.

Isao's expression hardened. "Why can't you be more helpful to your friends, Yaichi, instead of insulting them? Teppei's done so much for the hunting—"

"If you don't leave now, I'm setting the dog on ya," Yaichi said. His voice was like a growl.

"But, Yaichi—"

"You think I don't know how he bleeds money from old folks in the village, pretending like he's doing them a big favor by culling bears and wild boar that rip up the fields and woods round here?"

Isao bit his lip.

"And you and your mates get to pick up the crumbs, don-cha? The hunting club's a sham. And Teppei's a lame shooter who can't even train his dogs properly."

"Ya know, Yaichi, you take the cake. I always knew you were headstrong, but ever since Hatsue passed on, you're outta control."

Isao spat at his feet and got back in his car.

Noritsune barked.

"That's enough, Noritsune." Yaichi showed Noritsune his palm.

Noritsune instantly understood, though it was the first time Yaichi had used the gesture with him. He stopped barking and stood at Yaichi's side, glaring at the car as it disappeared down the road.

"Headstrong, am I?" Yaichi said in a disgusted tone. He grimaced as a sharp pain jolted down his back. He ripped open the painkillers he'd just bought and swallowed some without water. His body broke out in a greasy sweat. The drug would take a while to kick in. Nursing his pain, Yaichi hunched over and went inside the house. He kicked off his shoes in the entrance hall, crawled into the living room, and lay on the floor with a cushion under his head.

Noritsune stood in the entrance, watching Yaichi.

"Here." Yaichi thumped the floor beside him.

Noritsune cocked his head quizzically.

"S'okay. Come here." Yaichi thumped the floor again.

Noritsune jumped up the step into the house. Walking gingerly, he stepped into the living room and lay down at Yaichi's side. Until that moment, Yaichi had never once let a dog inside the living area. His belief was that in order to foster the kind of self-reliant spirit essential for any good hunting dog, it was best to make it live alone outside.

But Noritsune was not a hunting dog. Nor did Yaichi plan on training him as one. Besides, he was going to give up hunting soon. Warmth was what he needed now. Yaichi placed his hand on Noritsune's back. It felt warm. His pain subsided.

n no time, a month had gone by since Noritsune arrived. The autumn progressed, with the mountains turning red and yellow. Still, Noritsune's owner did not come forward. In the course of spending his days with the dog, Yaichi had grown to understand that Noritsune was on a long journey and that this was just a stop along the way, made necessary by his extreme hunger.

From spring through summer, there was no lack of food in the mountains of Japan. They were home to a bounty of small animals and fruit. But when fall came, the mountains became inhospitable. There was no fruit to be found, and all the small creatures disappeared from sight. Dogs hunted in packs, like their original ancestors, wolves, but there was a limit to what even the smartest and strongest of dogs could hunt down on its own.

After weeks of deprivation, Noritsune had eventually decided to accept food from a human hand. That was all well and good, Yaichi thought, but why come to him? He sometimes thought of Tamura's words: *Why'd he turn up here when there's all them houses in the village down below?*

At the time his answer had been because Noritsune was traveling through the mountains. But Noritsune would have come across any number of houses along the way. Why stop at his? Yaichi suspected that Noritsune had caught a whiff of death and loneliness. There was just something about the dog that made him think this.

Yaichi let Noritsune into the passenger seat of his mini truck and set off for town. He had upgraded the dog from truck bed to cabin, the same way he'd allowed him inside the house to sleep.

Noritsune sat in the front seat looking out the window. He seemed accustomed to being in a car.

"What kind of person was your owner? How'd you come to be separated?" Yaichi shot Noritsune the occasional question. He felt impelled to ask, though he knew he wouldn't get answers.

Yaichi noticed that Noritsune always faced the same direction: southwest. Like there was something to the southwest that was important to him. Was that where he was headed on his journey?

"Kyushu? You got family in Kyushu?"

Noritsune pricked up his ears but didn't move. He kept facing southwest.

Yaichi's bond with Noritsune had grown stronger in the past month, but whenever Noritsune faced southwest, he was like a different dog. A cold autumnal wind blew in the recesses of Yaichi's heart. Noritsune was his, but not his.

He could see the dog's yearning. And seeing it, he knew he should track down his owner in Kyushu and send him back to his rightful place. But he couldn't bring himself to do anything about it. The idea of being alone again at night was unbearable.

Yaichi hadn't always been like this. When he was young, he used to sleep alone under the stars for days at a time in pursuit of quarry up in the mountains. Not once had he pined for companionship.

Yaichi slowed the truck. He turned left at the intersection, then right. This brought him to the entrance of the town hospital's parking lot. He took a ticket and found a parking spot.

"Wait here," Yaichi said to Noritsune. He locked the car but left the windows open a crack. Though it was late autumn, the cabin would get hot in the strong sunshine. Leaving the windows open wasn't safe, Yaichi knew, but he doubted anyone would try breaking into a truck with a dog inside it.

He showed his card at reception, then went through to the internal medicine waiting area and sat down. He opened up a newspaper. Just like on TV, there was no decent news. Giving up on reading, Yaichi started doing the crossword.

"Mr. Katano, Yaichi Katano, please go to room two."

Yaichi stood up and entered the doctor's office. Dr. Shibayama, the internist, was staring at his computer screen. Yaichi took a seat.

"Mr. Katano," the doctor said, "these are the results from your last tests. I'm afraid they're not good. The cancer is progressing."

Yaichi nodded. He'd anticipated this, since he'd refused treatment.

"Won't you try chemotherapy? If you don't want that, at least check into the hospital."

Yaichi shook his head. "Just a prescription for painkillers, please."

"Mr. Katano—"

"As I said before, many times, no treatment. When the time comes, I'll just die."

Dr. Shibayama sighed. He'd been arguing with Yaichi about this ad nauseam, ever since finding cancer in his pancreas.

"Did you speak with your daughter?"

Yaichi shook his head.

"Mr. Katano, as I said last time, it's imperative to discuss it with your family."

"I know I'm making this hard for you, Doctor, and I'm sorry to make you fret over a selfish old codger like me."

"That's not the point." Dr. Shibayama frowned.

"I'll see you next month." Yaichi stood up.

"Is this really what you want?" the doctor asked, adjusting his glasses as he peered up at Yaichi.

"I gave it a lot of thought before deciding, Doctor. Thank you for seeing me today." Yaichi gave a deep bow and left the room.

Hatsue had also died of pancreatic cancer. She'd complained about not feeling well for a long time but didn't get around to having a checkup, so by the time she collapsed in pain and was taken by ambulance to the hospital, the cancer had already progressed to stage four.

Their only child, Misako, was married and living in Kyoto. She came straight home and took over all the decision-making. Including the use of powerful anti-cancer drugs. Misako behaved as if Yaichi wasn't even there. She didn't listen to his opinion and brushed off any word of complaint by saying he had no right to say anything.

Yaichi hadn't been a good husband or father. He had always been either off hunting in the mountains or out drinking. That was the kind of life he led.

I want to go home was Hatsue's constant refrain in the hospital. *I want to go home. I want to see Masakado.* All she wanted was to sit in the sun on the veranda, sipping green tea and enjoying some steamed sweet potato from her fields.

But her cancer-ridden body wouldn't allow her to move the

way she wanted, and the side effects of the drugs added to her suffering.

In the end, Hatsue wasted away in the hospital for almost a year before departing the world. She never went home or saw Masakado again.

I wish I could've died at home. Yaichi couldn't forget her last words as she looked into his eyes. *Why didn't you stand up to Misako for me?* those eyes seemed to ask. *Couldn't you have been a better husband, at least at the end?*

He saw the disappointment in her eyes. When she was well, he'd been nothing but a source of despair and disappointment to her, and it was the same when she died. From beginning to end, he had made Hatsue suffer. The thought of this caused him immense sorrow. When he learned that he had the same kind of cancer, he made up his mind immediately: no treatment.

He intended to spend his last days at home. This was where he would die, just as Hatsue had wanted to do. He would tend the fields she had devoted her life to, care for them until the last, and then die. He figured that was what Hatsue, too, would have wanted for him.

Even if Misako knew about his illness, it wouldn't be the same as with Hatsue. He could easily picture her contempt: *Do what you want, Dad.* Neither Hatsue nor Misako had forgiven him. Only the dogs did.

Yaichi picked up his prescription and paid the bill. On his way over to the truck, he saw the silhouette of Noritsune, sitting in the front seat. Facing southwest—no surprises there—and not stirring an inch. Anyone who didn't know better might have thought he was a statue. As he drew closer, Noritsune turned to face him. The corners of his mouth lifted. He was smiling. His tail was hidden, but Yaichi thought it was probably wagging.

"Sorry to keep you waiting," he said, stroking Noritsune's back as he settled himself in the driver's seat. "Let's go home. You wanna go for a walk up the mountain today? I gotta drop by the drugstore first, though. I'm almost out of painkillers."

Yaichi started the engine. His bouts of back pain were becoming more frequent as the weather grew colder. He had a feeling he wouldn't see the winter out. Before then, he needed to decide what to do about Noritsune.

"I know, but I won't die tomorrow," he said, stepping on the accelerator.

YAICHI STOOD WITH HIS hand on the trunk of the tree, repeatedly drawing air deep into his lungs. He and Noritsune had set out up the mountain not even an hour ago. Yet he was breathing heavily, and his knees were giving way.

"Geez, I'm pathetic," he couldn't help saying.

This time last year he had been racing along these trails with Masakado, in search of game. After Masakado died, he didn't go up into the mountains anymore. Even so, he never imagined his stamina could drop so much in only seven months.

When he was young, Yaichi only had to walk up a mountain to feel rejuvenated. At around age fifty, he started to feel like the less he went up into the mountains, the more his fitness declined. This breathlessness now, though, was not due simply to age. The disease was whittling away at his strength.

Up ahead, Noritsune waited on the other side of an animal track, looking back down at Yaichi. He didn't draw closer or move farther away. He was simply waiting for Yaichi.

Yaichi pulled a bottle of water from the side pocket of his backpack and took a swig. He felt the liquid seeping into every cell of his body, and his breathing settled.

"Wait. I'll be there in a sec."

Yaichi put the bottle back, then scanned the ground at his feet. He spotted a dry branch that he could use as a walking stick. He picked it up and set off again. It was a sorry day for him to be reduced to using something like this. Couldn't be helped, though.

He stabbed at the ground with his stick as he followed the animal track. This was the steepest part of the mountain. At the top of this slope, the ground leveled out. Yaichi gritted his teeth and breathed through his nose. He put one foot down after the other. His shirt felt uncomfortably wet with sweat.

It took a lot longer than he expected to reach the spot where Noritsune waited for him. The dog was sniffing keenly at every tree in the vicinity.

Yaichi also noticed there were traces of another animal. A wild boar and its piglet had been through here very recently.

"No chasing after it," Yaichi said.

Noritsune stopped sniffing and turned to look at him. Listening.

"A mother boar is a tough customer. You might be strong, but you'll have a hard time going up against a mother determined to protect her young. Best thing is to move away quietly."

Noritsune wriggled his nose and let the scent go.

"You really do have smarts. I wonder how you were trained," Yaichi said. Of course there was no answer. But this was Yaichi's method. Keep talking to the dog. He may not understand the words, but he will try to read the human's will. Speaking helped strengthen their bond, which could be worth everything if the chips were down. The bond between man and dog was priceless.

"Let's go," Yaichi urged Noritsune. He walked off ahead. The peak was only ten minutes away. This mountain wasn't that high, but Yaichi had cleared some of the vegetation around the top so he could enjoy the view.

Yaichi's breathing became more settled as he climbed the gentle slope, and his knees felt stronger. He didn't need the stick anymore but still kept a tight grip on it. He was bound to need it going down—descending put more strain on the leg muscles than going up did.

All of a sudden the view opened up. They had arrived at the peak. Yaichi seated himself on a tree stump and drank some more water. He pulled the Yukihira saucepan from his pack and poured Noritsune some too. When Noritsune had finished drinking, he stood at the center of the peak and turned to face southwest. The border with Yamaguchi Prefecture lay six miles to the south along the mountains. Across Yamaguchi and on the other side of the strait was Kyushu. If you went southwest as the crow flew, you would be somewhere in the Oita region.

"How'd you come to be separated from your owner?" Yaichi asked again. Noritsune raised his ears but didn't move.

"You've been wandering around a long time searching, huh?"

At last Noritsune turned to him. Yaichi thought he recognized loneliness in those deep black eyes.

"Must be somebody really important to you. S'okay, I get it. You can leave. Don't worry about me."

Noritsune cocked his head to one side.

"I'm talking about your real family. Course you wanna be with them. Whaddaya doin' hanging around with me?"

The moment the words came out of his mouth, Yaichi arrived at the answer himself. Noritsune was there to see him through to his death. Out of all the houses he could have gone to, he chose Yaichi's. Because, Yaichi believed, he scented death and loneliness there. That was why he had postponed the search for his family—to be at Yaichi's side when death came marching in. To ease his loneliness.

Bullshit. Dogs were dogs. Not people.

And yet, Yaichi was well aware that dogs had a special relationship to humans. Maybe it was God who sent them, or maybe Buddha. Who knew? But he knew they had been dispatched for the benefit of our foolish species.

They understood the human heart and were attuned to it in a way no other creature was.

"Noritsune, here, boy," Yaichi said, beckoning. Noritsune moved closer. Yaichi tapped his own thigh, and Noritsune laid his jaw on it.

"Thank you," he said, and stroked Noritsune's head. "I'm grateful, ya know."

Yaichi continued stroking Noritsune's head, as if he would never tire of it.

4

A bear was on a rampage through the village at the foot of the mountain, filling its stomach before winter hibernation. It had climbed the persimmon tree in Ichiro Sugishita's garden, eating and scattering all his fruit. It had plundered vegetable fields in the neighborhood.

Once there had once been an invisible line between the village and the mountain wilderness that animals never crossed. But the relentless creep of aging and depopulation saw generations of customary care of the land give way to neglect that eroded the line. As boundaries ceased to exist, mountain creatures increasingly began to appear in the village.

The villagers could handle a deer or a wild boar, but a bear was something else. The air was charged with unease. In any encounter with a bear, a human would inevitably come off worse. Injured, or left to die.

Noritsune was out in the garden. He started barking. A visitor had arrived.

Yaichi fought against the pain in his back to lift himself up. A few days earlier, the pain had become constant. The pain-killers were losing their effectiveness, and the pain returned after only a couple of hours. Yaichi had already used up his prescription and was making do with over-the-counter pain-killers. But these, too, had stopped working. The only thing preventing him from going to the doctor for another prescription was his certainty that he'd be admitted to the hospital.

Isao's car rolled into the yard at almost the same moment Yaichi reached the garden.

"Yaichi, I gotta request for your services," Isao said the moment he got out.

"I'm not in the hunting business anymore," Yaichi said.

"Don't say that. You're the best hunter in these parts. The hunting club needs ya. We can't do this without you."

"I'm not strong enough to go up the mountain anymore."

Isao blinked repeatedly at this. "Yaichi, you lost weight?"

"You only noticed just now, did ya?"

"Don't tell me . . ."

Yaichi nodded.

"Where?"

"Pancreas."

"Pancreas? Same as Hatsue?"

"She went to her death blaming me. S'prob'ly her farewell gift."

"Don't joke about something like that, Yaichi. What about the hospital?"

"I see the doc once a month."

Yaichi went back inside and sat down on a chair in the entrance hall. It tired him out to simply stand around. Isao and Noritsune followed him inside.

"What about chemo? Or radiation?"

Yaichi shook his head. "Not having treatment. I got prescriptions for painkillers, that's it."

"But you'll die."

"Isao, you know very well what a bad time Hatsue had. All she could say in the hospital was how she wanted to go home. She wanted to die at home too."

Isao cast his eyes downward. When Yaichi had been unable to get away from the fields or to take a break from hunting, it had been Isao's wife, Kumi, who had looked after Hatsue.

"So it's pretty bad, then?" Isao said after a while.

"I went up the mountain with Noritsune the other day. Took me more than an hour to reach the top."

Isao went pale. Yaichi used to be able to reach the top in less than half an hour.

"Didn't realize you was that bad."

"S'why I'm asking, leave me outta this bear business."

"So ya say, but nobody knows much about hunting bear. They've only shot deer and boar."

"Same as boar. Find the traces, track it, shoot. Anyways, I can't move, so I'd be useless."

"Ya really plan on not getting treatment?"

Yaichi nodded. "When the time comes, I'll just drop dead."

"What about the dog? If you die, he'll be on his own." Isao turned his head toward Noritsune.

"I got a favor to ask you about that, Isao," Yaichi said.

"Favor?"

"When I die, I want ya to take him to Kyushu."

"Kyushu?" Isao's eyes grew wide.

"Anywhere's okay. Just let him go somewhere up in the mountains in Kyushu. He should be able to find his own way after that."

"Whaddaya mean, 'find his own way'?"

"He's looking for his family. He just happened to drop by and see me on his way."

"Looking for his family? A dog?"

"Yup. He's that kinda dog. Isao, I'm begging ya. I never asked anything from you before, did I? Please, just do this for me."

"I don't mind, but . . ."

"Thanks, Isao." Yaichi gripped Isao's hand.

Isao clearly looked confused. As he should have been. He'd known Yaichi for more than thirty years, but Yaichi had never acted like this before.

"I'll do it, but make sure ya stick around as long as ya can, Yaichi. You only just turned seventy."

"I've lived long enough. Also, keep this a secret, will ya?"

"I don't mind. You've always been a hermit anyways. Nobody'd notice if you dropped dead all of a sudden."

Yaichi laughed. "You got it."

"Ya told Misako, huh?"

"Well . . ." Yaichi turned evasive.

"Ya gotta tell her. There's just you and her in the family— father and daughter."

"She hates me. She'll be happy when I kick the bucket."

"Nope, I'm not havin' it. You tell Misako, or else I won't do anything for the dog. If ya can't tell her yourself, I'll do it for ya."

"Isao—"

"Nope. I'm not givin' in on this. You gotta tell her. Promise me you will."

"All right. I'll phone her tonight," Yaichi agreed.

"If I hadn't come along, you really would've kicked the bucket without telling Misako, huh."

"I want to do this on my own."

Yaichi wouldn't have said anything to Isao, either, if Noritsune hadn't been there. Perhaps having Noritsune at his side was changing his fate. *Still, I'll be dying soon enough*, he thought, grimacing in pain.

"Well, I'll be on my way, then. You let me know if anything happens, right? Don't hold back. I'll do whatever I can."

"All right. I won't hold back anymore."

Isao gave a relieved smile and left.

Noritsune went over to Yaichi and pressed himself against his thigh. Yaichi stroked his back.

"It's a strange thing, but when I'm petting you, I don't feel the pain so much."

Yaichi closed his eyes and continued stroking Noritsune.

YAICHI'S CELL PHONE RANG. Most hunters nowadays had phones with map apps, GPS, and whatnot. But Yaichi was capable of moving through the mountains without depending on any of these. More often than not, he could also predict the weather more accurately than the TV forecast. Long years of experience aided his judgment.

If somebody depended on their phone apps, it was a sign they didn't have confidence in their own skills. That was why a regular cell phone was the only kind of device Yaichi carried, and even that was rarely used.

"Hello?"

"Dad?"

Yaichi heard Misako's voice. Isao must've told her anyway. "What's up?"

"I just had a call from Mr. Tamura."

"Oh."

"He told me you're not getting treatment."

"Oh." Yaichi stifled a sigh. Noritsune came over and rested his jaw on Yaichi's thigh. He stroked the dog's head.

"You think it was my fault that Mom suffered so much when she died, don't you?" Misako's voice was harsh. She was always like this. Yaichi couldn't remember her ever speaking gently to him since she went to high school. This, too, was something he had only himself to thank for.

"No, I don't."

"You think I made her have chemo against her wishes, don't you?"

"I said I don't."

"Then tell me why were you planning on dying alone, without getting treatment or telling me?" Misako all but yelled at him.

"I didn't want to cause you any trouble," Yaichi replied.

"Trouble? How can you say that? When you're my father— my only parent! And I'm your only child."

Yaichi wasn't expecting this. He shut his mouth.

"We don't get along, and I don't like you. But I've never once thought I wished you'd die. Do you get that? Even if I never see you, just the thought of you walking in the mountains with your gun makes me feel safe. If Mr. Tamura hadn't

called, you would've died all on your own, without me knowing a thing."

"I didn't want to make it hard for you," Yaichi said. His
voice was scarcely audible.

"Too late for that now, after all the grief you gave Mom
and me."

"I'm sorry." Yaichi bowed his head.

Noritsune stared at Yaichi curiously.

"I know I made mistakes with Mom too," Misako said. "She
so wanted to go home, but in the end I couldn't get her back
there. That's why I'm prepared to go along with whatever you
decide. But I can't pretend nothing's happening. I'll be there a
week from Saturday, with Kinu."

Yaichi hadn't heard his granddaughter's name in a long time.
Kinu would have started college by now. He'd heard she was
going to one in Osaka.

"Is Kinu well?"

"Disgustingly so. Make sure you keep yourself alive till we
get there. I'll never forgive you if you die on me before then."

"Okay, got it. You coming by car?"

"The train takes too long, and the nearest station is too far
away. I'll get Kinu to drive."

"Kinu can drive?"

"She got her license as soon as she started college. She drives
Kazuo's car on the weekends."

"Oh, really." Yaichi scratched his head. He didn't know anything about his own family. Little wonder, since he'd never bothered to find out.

"So, how are you?" Misako's tone shifted.

"Still doing all right," Yaichi lied.

"Okay. Well, I'll be there next week. I'll bring you some pickles that Kazuo's mother made. Mom used to love those. I'll put them on the altar, and you can have them afterward."

"Great. Those Nara pickles are a treat."

Misako's husband was from Nara. Every year Misako's mother-in-law sent homemade pickles. They were superb. Hatsue had always enjoyed them.

"Well, I'll see you soon."

"Yup."

The line went dead. Yaichi kept staring at the phone in his hand, as if bewitched. Eventually he put it away in the breast pocket of his shirt.

"People can be really dumb," he said to Noritsune. "And I take the prize for being the dumbest of all. You dogs are so smart, you probably can't believe it."

Noritsune snorted and moved away.

Yep, well and truly surprised, I bet, thought Yaichi. He smiled and stood up. That very instant, a stabbing pain surged down his back, and he fell into a heap. He lay facedown on the floor, breathing jaggedly.

Noritsune paced anxiously around him.

"It's okay." Yaichi lifted his head.

Noritsune stopped and brought his nose to Yaichi's face. He sniffed intently.

"Don't you worry. I won't die till Misako and Kinu get here."

After a while, the pain abated. Yaichi rolled onto his back and lay spread-eagle.

"A week from Saturday. Ten days from now. Shouldn't be any problem. Noritsune, you'll put in a good word for me with the gods, won't you? Let me have ten more days of normal life. You can ask that much for me, can't you? Seeing as how you dogs are messengers from the gods and all."

Noritsune clamped his teeth on the sleeve of Yaichi's jacket and pulled on it. *Get up, go and lie on the futon, not here*, he seemed to say.

"All right, all right." Yaichi took his time raising himself up. "You're just like Hatsue, nagging me not to sleep in the entrance hall or drink too much." He looked into Noritsune's eyes. "Could even be the spirit of Hatsue in there," he said, and went to the bathroom to brush his teeth.

5

The hunting club had failed to bring down the bear. Instead of making a clean kill, they only wounded it. Now the village was in a panic.

Teppei Nakamura had apparently brought in a hunter from Tamba, in Hyogo Prefecture, reputed to be a famous shooter. But the so-called famous shooter had botched the job. In a hurry to take the shot, he merely pierced the bear's flank. The animal fled at lightning speed, and the hunters lost its trail.

"What a mess," Yaichi said, shaking his head.

He washed down some painkillers with water and paused to take a breath. His medication was wearing off even more quickly now, and the pain got worse every day. Enough to force him back to the doctor for another prescription. He didn't want to hear all over again about being hospitalized and how it wasn't too late for treatment, but he couldn't have things entirely his way. He managed to get a prescription for a larger amount of pills by saying that he was too busy to come in for the next checkup. But he couldn't be sure that even all these pills would last long enough.

The over-the-counter pills had no effect whatsoever anymore. When his current prescription ran out, he would have to have a good talk with the doctor about what came next. But he wasn't going to the hospital. Or getting cancer treatment. That was final. All he wanted was guidance on how to manage the pain.

Noritsune turned toward the entrance and barked once, then kept staring at it. Yaichi heard a car approach. Isao, he guessed. Noritsune could tell the difference between the mailman's motorbike, the delivery service truck, and Isao's car.

"Yaichi, I'm comin' in to see ya." Isao let himself inside.

"Thought you'd turn up," Yaichi said.

Isao took one look at Yaichi and stood rooted to the spot. "Ya look terrible."

"S'cause I'm sick."

"Ya seein' the doc?"

"Day before yesterday."

"Now I'm really worried." Isao lowered himself onto the bench in the entrance hall. "Did ya hear about the botch-up yesterday?"

"Ya called in a crackerjack from Tamba?"

"Son of a bitch. I called the Tamba Hunting Club last night

and got laughed at. Turns out the swindler is all talk. S'all he's good at."

"You and Teppei are both off your game, getting taken in like that." Yaichi screwed up his lips.

"Ah, he wanted to make quick work of it, with the election getting close. Thought he'd get a boost by bringing down the bear. If you'd lent a hand, this wouldna happened."

"You saying it's my fault?"

Isao hastily shook his head. "Nope. Just hopin' ya can help out next time. You know well enough how dangerous the bear is now."

A wounded bear driven by rage and fear attacked everything in sight. This was why if it was necessary to shoot a bear, it had to be brought down with one shot.

"All the old folks in the village are in a panic. Some of 'em even sayin' they won't vote for Teppei."

"I'd like to help, but I'm afraid I can't," Yaichi said in a sardonic tone. "I doubt I could walk up the mountain, let alone hold a gun properly."

"Is it that bad? Shouldn't ya be in the hospital?"

"I'm all right at home. But up in the mountains I'd be a woeful case."

"So you really can't . . ."

"Sorry."

"Can't be helped, then, if you're sick. We'll deal with the bear somehow. Take care of yourself." Isao nodded and left.

Noritsune locked his eyes on Yaichi. *Are you really okay with that?* Yaichi felt he was being asked.

"Can't be helped. I'd only be a millstone up there." He turned his face away from Noritsune's gaze.

YAICHI UNLOCKED THE GUN safe and took out his M1500. Though he hadn't used it in a while, he was still keeping up with the maintenance. He took the rifle apart, cleaned it, and reassembled it. Holding it up in the shooting position, he squeezed the trigger. No problems there. Yaichi let out the air he'd been holding in his lungs.

He hadn't expected to ever use this gun again, but the time had come once more. Yesterday, Teppei Nakamura had led the hunting club into the mountains to cull the injured bear. Instead, the bear struck back, seriously injuring one of the club members.

"S'why ya gotta do the job properly the first time."

Yaichi got changed. He put on climbing pants and a flannel shirt, layered with a warm fleece and a multi-pocketed vest, its pockets stuffed with spare ammunition, a knife, a whistle, and various other items. Next, trekking shoes and his old, familiar gloves. Now he was ready.

"Noritsune."

When Yaichi spoke, Noritsune trotted over to his side.

"I haven't taught you anything about hunting, but you're a smart dog, so you'll catch on. Follow my orders, and you'll be all right. Got it?"

Noritsune looked up at Yaichi. His eyes were so clear it was unnerving.

"Once we get back from shooting the bear, you're free to go. You don't have to stay with me. You go off and find your owner."

Yaichi tapped Noritsune on the head, then went outside. They got in the mini truck and drove down to the village. The entire hunting club was already assembled, waiting in the parking lot of the local shrine. When Yaichi arrived, they swarmed over to greet him.

"Good of you to help, Yaichi. We're counting on you," Teppei Nakamura said. He was looking jittery. A man had been injured, and the hunting club had completely lost face. It was going to have an effect on the election.

"Like I said to Isao, you all go up to the peak and drive the bear down in the direction of Tsurudamari," Yaichi said.

Tsurudamari was a small pond located on an open stretch of ground halfway up the mountain. Migratory cranes used to stop there a long time ago.

"Will you be okay on your own, Yaichi?" Isao asked.

"Ehh, I prefer it," Yaichi said.

As far as Yaichi was concerned, the hunting club was a bunch of rotten shooters, hunters in name only. If any of them came with him, they would only be a liability.

"That fraud from Tamba went up on his own. Says he's gotta take responsibility for injuring the bear," Teppei Nakamura said.

"Why didn't ya stop him?" Yaichi asked sharply.

Teppei Nakamura scowled. "I tried. But he wouldn't listen."

"Not a great move, bringing someone like that along." Yaichi slung his gun from his shoulder. "Well, I guess he can't do much on a mountain he's got no experience with," he said. "You probably know this, but no talking—the only signal is a whistle. And don't let your dogs loose."

Everybody nodded.

"Let's get started, then. I'll be waiting at Tsurudamari."

The men went to make their way up the mountain. Their dogs were restless with excitement.

"For cryin' out loud, keep your dogs under control," Yaichi complained.

The men changed course and went in a different direction. Yaichi and Noritsune took an off-trail route, Noritsune automatically falling in line behind Yaichi.

Not five minutes had gone by before Yaichi regretted not bringing a walking stick. It was a twenty-minute walk to Tsurudamari. Yaichi had overestimated himself, thinking he could cover the distance unaided. His strength had weakened far more than he thought. His backpack and rifle were as heavy as lead. With every step up the slope, the muscles in his thighs trembled and his breath became raspy.

"I'm going to pot," Yaichi lamented to himself.

"So this is how people die," he turned around to say to Noritsune. "Only a year ago I was up and down this mountain in the snow. Now look at me."

Noritsune did not react. He simply kept sniffing the air.

"You're right. There's no time for griping—gotta get a move on."

Yaichi wiped the sweat from his forehead and drank some water. At this rate it would take him an hour to get to Tsurudamari. The hunting club would reach the peak and start moving down before he even arrived at the pond. He had to move faster. Gritting his teeth, he pressed on. His breathing became more rapid, and sweat dripped off him like a waterfall. His feet were like blocks of lead. His lungs felt on fire.

By the time Yaichi got to the pond, he was utterly spent. He collapsed to the ground in the shade of a large boulder and tried to steady his breathing. According to his watch, he was fifteen minutes behind schedule. By now the hunting club would have reached the peak and would be getting ready to drive the bear down the mountain.

Once his breathing was more settled, Yaichi did a slow

circuit of Tsurudamari. This was where the wildlife that lived on the mountain came to drink. He found traces of deer, boar, fox, and raccoon dog scattered about its edge, with a very fresh bear print in the mix.

The wounded bear had been here to drink.

But at the moment there was no sign of any animals. They would've all retreated at the first sign of the hunting club and would be hiding out somewhere, holding their breath.

From uphill came the sound of five-gallon drums. The men had scattered in all directions and were raising this racket on their way down to drive the bear toward Tsurudamari.

Yaichi went back to the shadow of the boulder and loaded his rifle.

"Noritsune, don't move for any reason," he ordered. He got down and lay on his belly. Then he took up his position with the rifle and got his breathing under control. Yaichi made his mind go blank. He became one with the mountain. This was the core tenet of his hunting philosophy. Don't raise suspicion in your quarry, make it feel safe, then take it down.

After a few minutes, Yaichi noticed movement in the thicket on the other side of the pond. He tensed his trigger finger, then immediately relaxed it again. There was something strange about the way the thicket was moving. It didn't look like the rustlings of a wild animal.

"It's that fraud from Tamba."

Clicking his tongue in disgust, Yaichi went to get up. If he didn't chase the intruder away quickly, the bear would sense something amiss and not come anywhere near here. But as he tried to stand up, he staggered. He lost his balance and stuck one hand out to grab hold of the boulder.

Across the pond, a silhouette emerged from the thicket. The hunter from Tamba.

Get outta here! Yaichi went to wave his arm, but in that same instant he felt a tremendous blow to his chest. Gunfire reverberated in his ears as he dropped to the ground. The hunter had mistaken Yaichi for a bear and shot him.

"Fucking idiot," Yaichi gasped, vomiting up blood.

Noritsune howled. A keen, powerful howl.

Yaichi felt no pain. Only cold. His hands and feet were rapidly becoming chilled. Was this how he was going to die?

Yaichi opened his eyes. A blue expanse filled his vision. The deep, clear blue of the winter sky. As clear and deep as Noritsune's eyes.

Yaichi had taken countless lives with his rifle. Now, thanks to that idiot, his own would be taken. *Retribution, I guess.* He meant to say this out loud but couldn't tell if he had.

He felt something soft on his cheek. Noritsune's tongue. Noritsune was licking Yaichi's face.

"You've done enough for me, Noritsune. I'm dyin'. Go find your owner." Yaichi raised one heavy hand to wave him away.

But Noritsune did not move. He stopped licking Yaichi's cheek and stood looking down at him.

"Aha. So this is why you turned up at my place. To see me off when I went."

Those eyes—they really were like the winter sky. Black, but deep and clear.

"I was expecting to die alone. Like I deserved. But you're here, Noritsune." Yaichi smiled. "Thank you," he said.

And then he took his last breath.

vi

The Boy
and the Dog

1

oru Uchimura slammed on his brakes. Up ahead, something had stumbled out onto the road from the forest.
A wild boar piglet? he thought. In that case, the mother
would be close behind. He needed to get past it and out of there
as fast as he could.

But the road was narrow, and the animal was right in the
middle of it. He honked his horn. With any luck, the noise would
scare off both mother and child. Instead, the piglet hunkered
down. No doubt frightened. Toru grumbled in irritation and
turned on the headlights. The mountain shadows made it especially hard to see in the already dim light of dusk.

"Huh?"

It was no boar. The animal caught in his headlights was a
dog. Thin. Dirty. Injured as well, it seemed.

Toru got out of the truck and approached it. "Hey there,
what's up? You hurt?" he asked it in a soothing voice.

The dog cast a quick upward glance at Toru. Its tail flapped. Like it was used to seeing people.

"Look at you, all skin and bones." Toru bent low and slowly brought his hand to the dog's muzzle. The dog licked his fingertips.

"You hurt? Okay if I take a look?"

The dog made no attempt to get up. Toru touched its body. Its fur was stiff and knotted. There were patches of caked blood too. It might have been attacked by a boar. Though its wounds didn't seem too serious, it looked roughed up, not to mention starving and exhausted.

"Wait a sec."

Toru went back to his truck and retrieved a bottle of water and the banana he'd bought for a snack. He offered the dog a drink. It caught the water from the tilted bottle with its tongue and gulped it down. Toru broke the banana into small pieces and fed the dog. Its tail continued wagging as it ate.

"You should see a vet. Okay if I take you?" Toru asked.

The dog closed its eyes. Taking this as a yes, Toru lifted it up. It weighed very little.

THE DOG LAY belly down on the examination table with its eyes closed.

"He's malnourished," said Dr. Maeda. A farmer Toru knew had recommended him. "But I don't think he's in any danger. I'll give him a drip, and we'll see how he does. He's also microchipped."

"Microchipped?"

"It's like an electronic tag under the skin. If I run the scanner over it, we can find out who his owner is."

"That'd be great. I'd like to get him back to his owner, if I can."

"Will do. Take a seat in the waiting room."

Toru left the examination room and stepped outside to make a call.

"Hey, it's me."

"Where are you? I was worried. I thought you'd had an accident." Despite her words of concern, Toru's wife, Sachiko, sounded calm.

"I found a dog on the way home."

"A dog?"

"Yeah. He's skin and bones. Can't even walk. I'm at the vet. He's getting a drip."

"A vet? That's not covered by insurance, is it? Isn't that expensive?"

Their finances were in a dire state. Toru could well understand why Sachiko might complain.

"Can't be helped. I couldn't just leave him there."

"You're right. You wouldn't be able to sleep at night if you had."

"Anyway, I think he'll be spending the night here. I'll be home once I've filled out all the forms. Go ahead and eat without me."

"Okay, then."

"How's Hikaru?" Toru inquired about his son.

"Same as usual. Drawing with his crayons. See you later."

"All right, bye, then."

He hung up and went back to the waiting room.

"Mr. Uchimura, you can go back in," the receptionist said.

Toru opened the door of the examination room.

"According to the microchip, the dog is from Iwate," Dr. Maeda said, staring at the computer screen.

"Did you say Iwate?"

"The city of Kamaishi. The owner is one Kazuko Deguchi. The dog is six years old this year, and his name is Tamon. I guess he was named after Tamonten."

Dr. Maeda tapped on the keyboard, and the printer started up. He handed Toru the piece of paper it spat out. "I wonder how he got from Iwate to Kumamoto. Will you contact the owner?"

"Yes, I'll do that." Toru looked down at the paper. It had a phone number and address in Kamaishi.

"HE'S FROM KAMAISHI?" Sachiko asked. She was cleaning up from dinner but stopped when Toru gave her the news. Without the noise of running water, the only sound was Hikaru's crayons scratching on paper in the living room. He was always drawing. Several pictures a day. His parents thought he drew animals but couldn't tell if they were dogs, cats, or something else. All they knew was that he drew animals.

"And you can't contact the owner?"

"No. I tried, but the number isn't in use anymore."

"How would he get here from Kamaishi?"

"Dunno."

"It's a strange coincidence, don't you think?"

Toru nodded. Kamaishi was where they used to live. Until, that was, it had been destroyed by the earthquake and the tsunami. Their home and fishing boat had been swept away. They'd done their best to get back on their feet, but Hikaru had developed a phobia of the sea. Then, four years ago, a distant relative helped them move to Kumamoto in Kyushu. The transition from fishing to farming hadn't been easy, and it was only recently that they were finally able to make a steady income.

"I contacted Yasushi and asked him to check out the address. See if anyone's living there."

Toru hadn't been in touch with his old fishing buddy for quite some time.

"Brings back memories of Kamaishi, doesn't it? I wonder how things are there now."

Since their move, they hadn't once gone back. Quite the opposite, in fact: they tried to keep the place out of their minds.

"What'll you do if we can't find the owner?"

"You said it yourself. It's a strange coincidence," Toru replied.

"Yes, I did. But how do you think Hikaru would take it?"

Sachiko's eyes turned toward the living room, where Hikaru was absorbed in his drawing.

2

Kazuko Deguchi was dead. Lost in the tsunami, according to Yasushi. She still had living relatives in Kamaishi, but apparently they did not want to take the dog.

After Toru finished his morning work in the fields, he returned to the vet. Tamon was caged in a back room. Upon noticing Toru, he lifted his head and wagged his tail. The drip had worked. He was looking much better than he looked the day before. His fur had been wiped clean and a sheen was visible now.

"He's recovering well. I'll keep an eye on him for one more day, and then he should be fine to leave," Dr. Maeda said. "I ran some other tests, and apart from malnourishment there's nothing wrong with him. He's got quite a few cuts, but they're almost all healed. I also gave him a rabies shot and other vaccinations, to be safe."

"Thank you. Apparently his owner in Kamaishi died in the tsunami."

Maeda pondered this. "Which means," he said, "that this

fellow has spent the last five years traveling from Kamaishi to Kumamoto."

"How could he have crossed the sea?"

"Dogs are excellent swimmers." Maeda smiled.

"Seeing as his owner is dead, I'd like to keep him, Doctor. Is there any problem with that?"

"None at all. Since the owner is deceased, this dog is effectively a stray. All you need to do to become the new owner is register him."

"Great."

"You can fill out the forms here. Do you want to say hello to Tamon first? He doesn't respond much to me or the nurse, but when you walked in, his tail started wagging. He trusts you."

Toru nodded. He walked over to Tamon's cage and crouched down.

"Yo, Tamon. I'm your new owner. Pleased to meet you."

Tentatively, he poked a finger through a gap in the cage. Tamon licked it and thumped his tail.

WHEN TORU WENT TO put a collar on Tamon, the dog recoiled. Clearly he did not like the idea.

"If you don't wear this, you can't live with me," Toru said in a soft voice.

Tamon looked at him. Drool trickled from his mouth.

"I won't do anything bad to you. I promise. You can trust me. Hey, I saved your life, didn't I?"

Tamon stopped backing away. Toru gently attached the collar.

"See. That was okay, wasn't it?"

He clipped on the leash and stood up. Cautiously, Tamon stepped out of the cage.

"Off we go." Toru nodded to Dr. Maeda and left the room. He settled the payment and completed all the paperwork.

Though Tamon was still extremely thin, his gait was firm. The vet had said that he seemed to be a mix of German shepherd and a native Japanese breed. Once he was back to normal, he should weigh somewhere between forty-five and sixty-five pounds.

Toru lifted Tamon and sat him in the passenger seat of the truck.

"Only till you get better. Then your place is in the back."

He stroked Tamon's head and went around to the driver's side. Tamon's nose twitched as he examined the scents in the cabin.

"Get better soon so we can go for walks." Toru patted Tamon once more, then drove off. Tamon turned to look out the window. Toru drove slowly so Tamon could take in the scenery. Once they were on the farm tracks, there was hardly any traffic.

Ordinarily the drive would have taken fifteen minutes, but today it took a half hour.

When Sachiko heard the truck, she came outside. "Hikaru, Tamon's here," she called into the house. Hikaru did not appear. *Lost in his own world as usual*, she thought.

Toru carried Tamon down from the truck. Immediately Tamon sniffed the ground, then approached Sachiko. She squatted down to watch him, letting him take the lead. He smelled her, then licked her cheek.

"Hi there. You like me?"

Tamon wagged his tail.

"You really are thin. We'll have to get some meat on you and get you well again. Okay?" Sachiko stroked Tamon's head, then rose to her feet. "First thing, though, is to give you a wash."

She already had a bucket and towel ready outside the house. Tamon was still not strong enough to be shampooed, so Sachiko had decided to simply wipe him down with a damp towel.

A sound came from the front entrance. Tamon turned to look. His tail started wagging frantically, with more energy than Toru had seen in him so far.

Hikaru emerged barefoot.

"Hikaru, put your shoes—" Sachiko's voice broke off.

Hikaru was staring directly at Tamon. Tamon's tail wagged

even faster. Hikaru broke into a smile. With a grin that split his face from ear to ear, he walked up to Tamon and touched him behind the ears.

Toru swallowed hard. He had not seen Hikaru smile since the tsunami.

ON THE THIRD DAY in the evacuation center, Sachiko had raised the alarm about Hikaru. "He doesn't say a word or even smile. He doesn't cry or get angry."

They attributed it to shock. The experience they had just been through was so traumatic, even adults were beside themselves with terror. What must it have been like for a three-year-old? It would resolve itself in time, they told themselves. Besides, what with the post-disaster chaos and life at the evacuation center, they couldn't find a doctor for Hikaru. They did everything else they could think of. Spoke to him frequently, tried to play with him. But he remained mute, and his face never showed any emotion. Paper and pencils were the only things that drew a spark of interest from him. He began drawing pictures. Day after day, picture after picture. Of what, however, his parents had no idea.

A month passed before they managed to get him to a specialist. In a borrowed car they drove to Sendai to see a child psychiatrist. The doctor's diagnosis was no different from his parents': shock. The trauma of the disasters had triggered something in Hikaru's mind. It should resolve in time, the doctor told them.

Another month went by. Then three more months. Still, Hikaru would not speak. All he wanted to do was draw. The doctor recommended various therapies, but nothing worked.

Then one day the family went down to the port for the first time since the tsunami. Toru and Sachiko had heard it was a grim sight but wanted to see it with their own eyes. The smell of burning lumber still hung in the air. Piles of debris dotted the area, and the roads were blocked by fishing boats carried inland by the waves.

Toru had been holding Hikaru in his arms. Just like he had held him on the day of the earthquake, as he ran for dear life toward higher ground to escape the tsunami. Hikaru's eyes were squeezed tightly shut. *Perhaps he's reliving that day*, Toru had thought.

As they got closer to the ocean, they could hear the waves. The smell of salt grew stronger, gradually overpowering that of burned wood. Hikaru was restive in Toru's arms. He opened his mouth wide and let out a scream. Piercing and high-pitched. Toru's ears nearly burst.

They turned on their heels and hurried away from the port. But it was a long time before Hikaru stopped screaming. That night he moaned and cried in his sleep. The silent reproach of others in the evacuation center drove Toru and Sachiko to take him outside and wait for dawn.

Ever since, Hikaru screamed whenever they went near the sea and had nightmares afterward. It didn't take long for Toru and Sachiko to decide to move. Far away from the ocean.

3

Hikaru was constantly by Tamon's side. At night he wanted Tamon to be with him when he slept. Tamon's fur still had ground-in dirt despite the towel wipe-down. Normally Sachiko would never permit a dog in that state to sleep in the same bed as Hikaru. But the smile on Hikaru's face trumped every objection.

Tamon was well-mannered. He never made a mess inside the house. In fact his behavior made it seem like he was used to living inside.

At the time of the tsunami, Tamon would have been a puppy. Had somebody been taking care of him, Toru wondered, since Kazuko Deguchi died?

The boy and the dog were never apart for a second. During the day they were always outside, soaking up the sun side by side or walking around the modest-size garden. Tamon's weight increased day by day, as if Hikaru's affection was as nourishing as the recovery diet recommended by Dr. Maeda.

Since Tamon's arrival, Hikaru had stopped drawing. He

smiled often but still did not talk. These smiles were directed at Tamon, who smiled back. Hikaru and Tamon were like a core of brightness in the old wooden house. The once-gloomy atmosphere lifted overnight, as if all of a sudden the house were getting more sun.

Toru and Sachiko observed Tamon accepting Hikaru's affection. It warmed their hearts.

"Tamon's like a gift from the gods, isn't he?" Sachiko said.

"He certainly is our angel," Toru agreed.

Toru was watching Hikaru play with Tamon in the garden. Hikaru would throw a ball, and Tamon would run after it, pick it up, and bring it back. Every time Tamon retrieved it, Hikaru patted his head and back. Tamon's reaction was to thrust his chest out proudly.

Toru was struck by a thought: maybe Hikaru and Tamon had known each other in another life. That was how close they seemed to be. They were like old souls who had found each other, or a couple falling in love at first sight. Their bond was ironclad, their trust in each other absolute. If one died, the other could not survive. Toru shook his head. *Don't go there*, he told himself. *They're having a great time. Just look after them.*

"Toru . . ." Sachiko called. She had both hands clapped over her mouth and her eyes pinned on Hikaru.

"What is it?" Toru followed her eyes. At some point Hikaru and Tamon had finished playing with the ball. Hikaru was sitting on the edge of the veranda with Tamon lying next to him, resting his jaw on Hikaru's thigh. Hikaru's eyes were screwed up tight in concentration as he stroked Tamon's head.

"Ta-mon," Toru and Sachiko heard. Actually heard the word. And saw Hikaru's mouth move.

Toru gripped the mug of tea he had been about to bring to his lips.

"Hikaru's talking," Sachiko said in a hoarse voice.

"Shhhh," Toru warned. He listened intently.

"Ta-mon." Hikaru's lips shaped the sounds.

"Hikaru, what did you just say?" Toru edged closer to Hikaru, who turned toward his father.

"Tamon." His mouth formed the word.

"That's right. Tamon. His name is Tamon."

"Tamon. Tamon. Tamon."

"Yes. Tamon. Can you can say Tamon's name, Hikaru?" Hikaru nodded.

Toru turned to Sachiko. "Hey, Hikaru spoke."

Sachiko nodded. Her cheeks were wet with tears.

ONE NIGHT, a week after Tamon came to live with them, Yasushi Akita called.

"Sorry about the other day. Hope it wasn't too much trouble," Toru said.

"Hey, it was nothing. So how's it going with the dog? Getting on okay?"

"Hikaru spoke," Toru replied.

"He did? No shit."

"He only says the dog's name. But it's a big step. We're really grateful to Tamon."

"Wow, he says the dog's name . . ."

"Can't keep 'em apart. Hikaru's always smiling at Tamon."

"That's great."

"Yeah. If it keeps up, we hope he might be able to go to school."

"Hearing you so happy makes me happy, too, buddy. Hey, listen, you couldn't take a photo of the dog, could ya, and email it to me?"

"A photo of Tamon? What for?"

"Heard an odd story, that's all. I wanna check it out."

"What'd ya hear?"

"I'll tell you if it checks out. For now, just send me a photo?"

"Sure, no problem, but—"

"Hey, you oughtta visit sometime. I'll get the guys together, and we can have a drink."

"Yeah, you're right, I should. I'll think about it. Catch you later, then."

Toru hung up and went to Hikaru's bedroom. Hikaru was asleep. He slept well these days. Playing with Tamon probably tired him out a lot more than drawing pictures ever had.

Tamon lay alongside Hikaru. When Toru entered the room, Tamon lifted his head. To Toru it looked like Tamon was there more to keep watch over Hikaru than to sleep.

"Don't mind me." Toru turned on the light and took a photo with his phone. "I guess this'll do." He checked the screen, then turned off the light. Once outside the room, he texted the photo to Yasushi.

"Wonder what story he heard." Toru shook his head. He could not for the life of him imagine.

4

Dr. Maeda had given Tamon a clean bill of health, and Toru was planning to take him out for a walk. Naturally, Hikaru, too, wanted to go. It had been a long time since he'd left the house for any reason other than to see a doctor.

Tamon didn't resist the collar or the leash. They left the house, Tamon walking on Toru's left, and continued up the road for ten minutes to the fields. Then they turned off the public road and onto the narrow farm vehicle track that bisected the expanse of rice paddies. There was no traffic here. Hikaru ran ahead, then turned to look back. He thrust his hand out at Toru.

"You want to hold the leash?" Toru asked.

Hikaru said nothing. He looked up unblinking at his father. Eyes alight with hope.

"Okay, Tamon?" Toru looked down at Tamon. He saw the same light in Tamon's eyes as in Hikaru's. Toru crouched low to look directly at Hikaru. "Whatever you do, don't let go of the leash, understand?" Toru said, then put the leash in Hikaru's hand.

Hikaru could not contain his joy. His face broke into an enormous smile. "Tamon," he called.

Tamon wagged his tail enthusiastically. He bounded up to Hikaru's side.

"Tamon," Hikaru called again, and walked off. Tamon trotted beside him, matching his pace to Hikaru's. They could have been longtime walking partners.

Toru hung back to watch them. Putting on weight had certainly given Tamon's bearing a certain grandeur. Looking at him, Toru felt sure that if anything were to happen to Hikaru, Tamon would be there for him.

Toru breathed in deeply and filled his lungs with air. He felt the stirrings of spring. The rice paddies were already filled with water and ready for planting. The surface reflected clouds in the expanse of blue sky. Toru listened to the murmur of a nearby mountain stream. March in Kamaishi was still winter, but here in Kumamoto the days were already warm and pleasant. Toru watched as Hikaru and Tamon walked through this landscape bursting with new beginnings.

Never thought I'd see such a sight, he thought. He and Sachiko had exhausted what they thought had been every possible option they could think of for Hikaru, and he could not deny that at some point resignation had set in.

Hikaru wasn't capable of leaving the house, let alone going to school. At this rate, all he would ever be able to do was draw. Toru had begun to conclude that he and Sachiko would just have to accept Hikaru as he was. That all they could ever hope for him was to lead a modest life with his family.

But look at him now. Out walking in the world. Smiling and bathed in the spring sunshine. Tamon walking affectionately by his side.

Toru wondered if he was dreaming. Everything that had happened—his finding Tamon, the scene in front of him now—was it all in his head? He was afraid he might open his eyes and find everything back to how it used to be. He shook his head, as if to snap himself out of his reverie.

Hikaru had suffered a long time, but now the gods had extended him a helping hand. Tamon was their messenger. *I should be grateful*, Toru thought, *just to see Hikaru smiling and playing with Tamon.*

"Hikaru," Toru called to Hikaru's back.

Hikaru turned around. Until now he had never reacted when Toru or Sachiko called him.

"Come and look at our paddy."

The Uchimuras grew rice on a half-acre plot rented from the local agricultural co-op. The yield was too much for a three-person family, but friends in Kamaishi were happy to receive the surplus. They chose to use natural rice-farming methods, out of concern for what would go into Hikaru's mouth. Most of the rice in the surrounding fields was farmed the same way. Grown for personal consumption, with little use of agricultural chemicals.

Toru took Hikaru's hand and led him along the dirt footpath between the paddies. If this were somebody else's field, he'd take care not to let Hikaru play there, but since it was his own, there was no problem. The far side of the paddy was in a shallow valley and had a path alongside it wide enough for a mini truck. Toru led Hikaru and Tamon over to it and removed Tamon's leash.

"There you go, Tamon. Have fun. You, too, Hikaru."

Tamon charged off. He ran a few yards, then stopped and turned to look back, as if inviting Hikaru to follow. Hikaru got the message and ran after him. Tamon spun around and sped away. Every now and then he looked back to check on Hikaru and adjust his speed.

"Smart Tamon," Hikaru cried, chasing after him. Their images were reflected in the mirrorlike surface of the paddy field as they ran.

This is happiness, it suddenly dawned on Toru. *We're happy again. At last, after five years.*

Toru walked around the edge of the paddy while keeping one eye on Hikaru and Tamon. When May came, it would be time to plant the rice seedlings. Then the battle against weeds would begin. It was tiring work, but he had a feeling that this year it would be a lot more enjoyable.

Hikaru caught up with Tamon and threw his arms around his back. Tamon had deliberately slowed down. Hikaru seemed delighted. Tamon equally so. Hikaru looked back at his father, then lifted his hand and waved.

"Come." Hikaru sounded the word. "Come . . . here."

A lump formed in Toru's throat.

"You talking to me? Are you asking me to go over there, Hikaru?"

"Come . . . here."

"Here I come." Toru wiped his eyes and broke into a run.

"HE SAID 'MOM.'" THEY were sitting at the table. Sachiko had her chin propped on her hands and a dreamy expression on her face. "You heard him too."

During dinner, Hikaru had addressed her as *Mom*. Just once. But there was no mistaking it.

"I never thought this day would come. It's like a dream." Sachiko looked content. When Toru opened another can of beer, she didn't even raise an eyebrow.

Tamon came into the living room. Hikaru had already brushed his teeth and gone to bed. Recently, Tamon had started coming out to the living room once Hikaru was asleep.

"Is he sleeping?" Toru asked.

In response, Tamon rested his jaw on Toru's thigh.

"Okay, I get it. You came out to be petted."

Apparently, Tamon saw himself like an older brother. He watched over Hikaru whenever the boy was awake, but once Hikaru went to sleep, he shed that role and came to Toru or Sachiko for petting.

Toru gently stroked Tamon's head.

"Tamon, I'm going to cook you a steak one of these days. As a reward for what you've done for Hikaru," Sachiko said.

Tamon gave a big wag of his tail.

"Hey, that's not fair. I'm the one who brought Tamon home. How about a steak for me too?"

"You've got your beer."

"Beer or steak? There's no comparison."

At that moment Toru's phone rang. He reached for it with a smile. It was Yasushi.

"Hey there. What's up? Did you find out anything from the photo I sent?"

"Get ready for this, Toru—you're not gonna believe it." Yasushi sounded excited.

"What?"

"Hikaru and the dog, Tamon. They knew each other when you lived here."

"What? How could they?" Toru sat up straight.

"Sada used to take Hikaru to play in that park near the port, didn't she?"

"Yeah," Toru agreed.

Sada was short for Sadako, Toru's mother. She used to baby-sit Hikaru in the daytime, when money was tight and Sachiko had taken a part-time job at the supermarket.

"Apparently this Kazuko Deguchi also used to go to that park a lot. When she was out walking Tamon."

"Are you serious?" Toru's hand holding his phone shook.

Sachiko stared at Toru with a puzzled expression. Tamon's jaw was still perched on Toru's thigh.

"There's this old guy I know who spent a lot of time in that park. He used to chat with Sada. Then when you told me you found a dog called Tamon, I remembered something he'd said. A long time ago. How one day Sada was there with the boy when a middle-aged woman came along with a puppy. And the boy and the puppy immediately hit it off. He said you could see it clear as day. Kids and dogs are so innocent, they can't hide their feelings."

"You're not saying . . . The puppy's name . . ."

"Yep, it was Tamon. Kinda unusual name. That's why the old guy mentioned it."

Toru's mouth went dry.

"S'why I asked for a photo. When I showed it to him, he said he thought it was the same dog. Seems he once asked the owner what kind it was, and she told him it was a cross between a German shepherd and a native Japanese breed."

"So you're telling me that Tamon made friends with Hikaru five years ago and came all the way from Kamaishi to find him?"

Surely not. How could a dog know where they'd moved? Dogs could track scents, but there was a limit to how far.

"Weird, eh? But you gotta say, it does look like the dog went looking for Hikaru, seeing as he was the person he liked most after his owner."

"No way that could be true."

"The dog's microchipped, isn't it? And the information says its name is Tamon from Kamaishi, right? If it was one when it met Hikaru then their ages are right too. Plus it's a mix of shepherd and Japanese. Tamon's got shepherd blood in him, doesn't he?"

"All true, but . . ."

Toru glanced at Tamon. He had filled out a lot and must weigh almost sixty-five pounds by now. When Toru had found him, though, he wasn't much over thirty pounds, and he had wounds all over his body. How was it possible he had traveled the length of Japan looking for Hikaru and appeared out of nowhere in front of Toru's mini truck?

"How about I give you the old guy's number? You can ask him for yourself," Yasushi said.

"Okay," Toru replied.

· · ·

YASUSHI'S ACQUAINTANCE WAS A retired fisherman named Shigeo Tanaka. Toru vaguely remembered him. He'd lost his home in the tsunami and was now living in Sendai with his married son. When Toru rang, Shigeo sounded eager to talk.

According to Shigeo, Tamon and Hikaru had first met early in the fall of 2010. As usual, Shigeo had been having a smoke on a bench in the park when Sada came along with Hikaru. She'd said hello and put Hikaru on the swing, which he loved. Sada stood pushing him and chatting with Shigeo. Then Kazuko Deguchi came walking by with a pup. Normally she went straight past the park, but that day the pup kept pulling on its leash, trying to drag her inside.

"The pup made a beeline for little Hikaru," Shigeo told Toru.

Kazuko was a bit embarrassed about its behavior, but when Hikaru saw the dog, his face lit up.

"Bow wow, bow wow," he'd said, jumping off the swing and going up to the pup.

"They were quite a sight—like a reunited couple. Sadako and Kazuko and me all said so when we talked about it later. Things like that can really happen. We all believed it."

From then on, Kazuko took the dog to the park every day except when it was raining or snowing. Hikaru and Tamon played in the sandpit, sticking close to each other's side.

"I'm not one for remembering names, but I couldn't forget that pup's. Tamon. After Tamonten. Apparently when he was born, his face reminded Kazuko of a Bishamonten statue she had in her house. So she called him Tamon."

Toru recalled that Bishamonten and Tamonten were two different names for the same deity. He was called Bishamonten when worshipped on his own and Tamonten as one of four kings who protected the four cardinal directions of Buddha's realm. Tamonten was guardian of the north.

"Sadako was excited about little Hikaru and Tamon being friends. Didn't she tell you?"

"No, not in so much detail." Toru remembered hearing that Hikaru had made friends with a puppy. But hardly more than that. Sachiko didn't remember much either when he had checked with her after Yasushi's call. At the time it had been a daily struggle for them simply to earn enough money to put food on the table. Toru couldn't afford to pay attention to everything his mother said.

When winter came, Sadako stopped taking Hikaru to the park every day. But she still went when the weather was warm enough, because Hikaru was always badgering her about wanting to see Tamon.

Kazuko continued to take Tamon to the park. Apparently he used to pull on his leash until she gave in and headed in that direction. It didn't make any difference telling him that Hikaru

wasn't there. Tamon was usually obedient, but when it came
to Hikaru, he got excitable.

Shigeo used to run into Kazuko and Tamon quite often. *I
don't know why he's so attached to little Hikaru*, Kazuko told him.

"There's no rhyme or reason when it comes to feelings. It
was love at first sight for them. They just hit it off. That's what
she said," Shigeo explained to Toru.

"Kazuko and Tamon had a good relationship too. You could
tell their bond was strong. If it hadn't been for the disasters . . ."
Shigeo sighed and fell silent.

Toru waited quietly for Shigeo to continue.

"I happened to see Tamon one day when I was staying at the
evacuation center. Must've been a month after the tsunami. I
called out to him, but he just took off. Maybe he didn't hear
me. He was probably searching for Kazuko. By then I'd heard
that she was missing, so I felt sorry for the pup. The next day I
went down to the park. It was all torn up. Not much of a park
anymore after the tsunami had ripped through it. But like I
thought, Tamon was there."

Shigeo went on to tell Toru how he'd seen Tamon staring
at the spot where the sandpit used to be. No doubt he was fret-
ting about Hikaru. Shigeo had spoken to Tamon and told him
that Kazuko had gone to heaven. Tamon didn't move an inch.
Shigeo was racked with pity at the sight of him—he looked so
brave and wretched—and wanted to take Tamon with him.

But he couldn't because he was living in the shelter, and pets weren't allowed. Instead, he managed to scrounge up some food to take to the park and feed him.

"He was starving. I couldn't get hold of much. Rice balls, that kind of thing, that was all. But he wolfed down whatever I gave him."

Shigeo had asked around, hoping to find out Sadako's whereabouts. If Kazuko was no longer in this world, he wanted to find Hikaru, the one other person he knew Tamon loved more than anyone.

"I couldn't believe it when I heard Sadako was dead too. I knew she had a son, but I didn't know your name. So hers was the only name I could give when I put the word out."

Tamon had lost Kazuko and couldn't find Hikaru. Still, he kept showing up in the park every day.

"About two months after I first saw him—the end of May, I guess it was, seeing as how the cherry blossoms had already fallen—Tamon stopped turning up."

Shigeo kept going to the park day after day, but Tamon never returned. For all his steadiness, Tamon was still a pup, less than a year old. Shigeo feared he'd gotten hurt and died. The thought broke his heart. But then it struck him: any dog that could survive an earthquake and a tsunami like that wouldn't die so easily. He would have bet anything that Tamon had gone in search of Hikaru.

He left the park for the last time, convinced that Tamon was still alive.

"I never saw Tamon again. In fact, I'd clean forgotten about him. But then, blow me down if he didn't really go off and track down little Hikaru in Kumamoto." Shigeo sighed loudly. "You coulda knocked me over with a feather. But it was like I thought all along. Tamon's the kind of dog you'd expect could do it. Besides, he loved Hikaru more than anything."

Toru thanked Shigeo politely and hung up.

"CAN THAT TAMON REALLY be the same as ours?" Sachiko asked after Toru told her what he'd heard. Her eyes were round in surprise.

"He is," Toru affirmed.

"What a dog . . ." Sachiko lowered herself onto the tatami and beckoned Tamon. When he came over, she wrapped her arms around him.

"What did you go through coming all this way? What was in your head that made you keep going? Finding Hikaru—was that it? Why do you love him so much?"

Tamon tilted his head to one side, then licked Sachiko's cheek.

"I have an idea . . ." Toru said, still forming the thought.

"What?"

"I should post something on social media. A photo of Tamon with a write-up about him coming all the way from Kamaishi to Kumamoto. Maybe somebody can tell us what happened in between. Someone must've seen him. I can ask people to share the post."

"A post on social media? Why would you do that?"

"I can't imagine Tamon got here all by himself. It took him five years. Somewhere along the way, somebody had to've taken him in for a while, or traveled with him. Dogs and wolves are animals that live in packs. Just one on its own would have a hard time getting enough food to survive. I don't think Tamon could have kept starvation at bay by himself for five years. Somebody must have fed him."

"I wonder if you'll find anything. I mean, nobody could know his name is Tamon unless they'd read the microchip."

"We won't know unless I try. Don't you want to know? Where he's been? What he was doing the last five years? How he managed to find Hikaru in Kumamoto? If it's possible to find out anything, Hikaru would want to know too."

"You're right. He would want to know."

Sachiko gave Tamon another hug.

5

oru's post failed to turn up anything. The most he got was the occasional nuisance comment or somebody mistaking Tamon for another dog. He told himself it was worth a try. That it was better than doing nothing. All the same, Toru couldn't help being disappointed at the complete lack of response. He had a sense he was missing something.

The post may have gone nowhere, but life continued to be good. More than anything, Toru and Sachiko were thrilled that Hikaru had started talking. His vocabulary was smaller than that of other children his age, but it was increasing day by day.

"What's this called?" was his favorite phrase. He insisted on asking the name of everything in sight and tried to memorize it—anything from food on the table to weeds on the side of the road. And he was able to express his will in everyday conversation with his parents, even if not with perfect grammar.

He also started drawing again. The subject of his pictures was still the same, but now they knew what it was: Tamon. All along, every picture he had ever drawn had been of Tamon. They realized that now. Not a cat, or a dog, or some other kind of creature. Tamon.

On the day of the earthquake and tsunami, Hikaru's mind had frozen in terror and remained so ever since. The one beam of light to have broken through to him were memories of Tamon and his unconditional love. So Hikaru had kept drawing pictures of him. Toru and Sachiko were convinced that was the reason. They fell into the habit of giving Tamon a hug every night before turning in. It was their small ritual of appreciation for the one who had pulled Hikaru out from the darkness. His savior.

Tamon was not wholly averse to being hugged. He wagged his tail and returned to Hikaru's bedroom once the ritual was over.

At night, Toru liked to gaze at the sight of the boy and the dog sleeping side by side. It was like something out of a religious picture. He often took a photo of them like that. One day, he would ask Hikaru to draw a picture based on these photos.

THE HOUSE WAS SHAKING. Hikaru's screams rang out. The tremors grew stronger. Toru made a dash for Hikaru's bedroom, struggling to keep his balance as he went. This quake was a big one. His mouth went dry. The trauma of the last one was still a fresh memory.

"Hikaru!" Toru cried out as he burst into the room. He could see Hikaru's tearful face in the light spilling in from the hallway. Tamon was standing at full height in front of Hikaru. Like a shield.

"It's okay, Hikaru. It's only an earthquake. The sea's a long way off. There won't be any tsunami," he said, picking up his son. Hikaru trembled violently in Toru's arms.

"It's okay, it's okay. Mom and Dad are here with you. Tamon's protecting you too."

"Tamon?" Hikaru stopped crying.

"Yes. Look, he's right there. Protecting you. There's nothing to be afraid of if Tamon's here, right?"

Hikaru nodded. The next moment, the lights went out. A blackout. Hikaru let out another high-pitched scream.

"Sachiko, bring me a flashlight," Toru yelled, clutching Hikaru tightly.

"It's okay. It's just a blackout." He spoke to Hikaru in a soothing voice. But Toru himself was nearly in a state of panic. What the heck? They had come here to get away from earthquakes and tsunamis, yet here they were in the middle of another quake just as bad. Were they cursed?

As Toru's mind raced, he felt something warm against his legs. Tamon. Tamon was pressed up against him. It seemed to him as if that sturdy muscular frame were sending out a message. *No need to fear. You're the boss of the house—act like it.* Toru nodded. It was his job to protect his family. Sachiko, Hikaru, and Tamon. This was no time to panic.

A light drew closer. Sachiko had reached them with a flashlight.

"Toru . . ."

"In here, quick."

Hikaru's room contained nothing other than his bed. That meant there was no danger of injury from toppling furniture. Nevertheless, Toru pulled a quilt over Sachiko and Hikaru, just in case.

"Keep still. Don't move till I get back. Got it?"

The rocking was starting to subside. But they couldn't afford to let down their guard yet. That was the lesson they had learned the last time. An earthquake didn't end at just one tremor.

It was pitch black outside. The whole village was without electricity. Toru turned to look in the direction of Kumamoto city and saw that it was dark over there too. He looked for signs of fire. No sign of that. *Good.* After the last earthquake, fires had started all over the place.

Toru picked his way to the mini truck, started the engine, and tuned the radio to NHK. Kumamoto had experienced violent levels of seismic intensity, while in Mashiki it was extreme, the announcer reported. The whole prefecture had been struck.

There is no danger of a tsunami from the earthquake. The instant Toru heard these words, his body relaxed. Logically he knew that even if there were another tsunami, it was geographically impossible to reach this far. Yet the instinctive fear was there.

He parked the truck closer to the front door and went back inside the house. By now the shaking had almost stopped.

"Come outside. We'll go to the community center."

This was their closest designated emergency evacuation shelter. The concrete-reinforced building would be able to withstand the earthquake better than the Uchimuras' wooden house.

"Hurry."

Sachiko threw off the quilt covers and left the bedroom with Hikaru in her arms. Tamon followed. Toru went to the living room and gathered up his wallet, bankbooks, and name seals before leaving the house.

Sachiko and Hikaru sat in the passenger seat, while Tamon was in the truck bed.

"Off we go." Toru handed the bankbooks to Sachiko and drove off.

People in their neighborhood were standing around outside. Though their faces were apprehensive, there didn't seem to be much of a sense of urgency. Nor did anyone else seem to feel the need to evacuate.

"Mr. Tanahashi." Toru slowed the truck as he approached

their elderly neighbor. "You should evacuate. There'll be aftershocks. Your house might be fine now, but not after a few more tremors. There might be landslides, too, down the hills at the back."

But Toru was pooh-poohed. "Nah," his neighbor said. "Won't get that bad."

"Don't say I didn't warn you." Toru stepped on the gas pedal. Anyone who hadn't experienced a major quake had no idea how terrifying it could be.

Sachiko tut-tutted in disapproval. "Why doesn't he leave?"

Light from the villagers' flashlights receded in the rear-view mirror.

A SECOND VIOLENT TREMOR struck in the early hours of the morning. The Uchimura family, along with others taking shelter in the community center, heard on the battery-operated radio that the aftershock was also of a magnitude of around six.

Their fears grew. Could their old wooden house withstand the continuing onslaught? Were Tanahashi and their other neighbors all right?

Hikaru could not stop trembling despite Sachiko's and Tamon's efforts to comfort him. Dogs weren't allowed inside the community center, but they had received permission to bring Tamon inside after explaining the situation. Because there were not many people in the hall, they were told. And he would be allowed to stay only until the morning.

Morning came, and Toru had still not slept a wink. There had been an occasional small tremor during the night but no other major aftershocks. They would come, however, though gradually diminishing in scale and frequency.

By morning, Hikaru was calmer. The radio told of widespread damage. Not surprisingly, the town of Mashiki had been hit worst. Damage there was immense.

After a breakfast of Cup Noodles and rice balls prepared by the staff at the center, Toru decided they would return home. He expected the aftershocks to settle down, and of course there would be no tsunami here. It wasn't possible that they could experience a second full-course banquet of earthquake, tsunami, and fire within five years.

Back in the village, everybody was busy cleaning up. Fortunately, there didn't appear to be any houses destroyed by the quake. But there was still no power or water.

As the Uchimuras had anticipated, the inside of their house was chaos. Crockery shelves, bookshelves, and chests of drawers lay toppled, while the floor of the living room and kitchen were so strewn with broken china that there was no place to set foot. But the house was still standing. It hadn't been swept away by a tsunami or consumed by fire. They were happy simply to have a roof and four walls to keep out the wind and rain.

Toru and Sachiko divided the work between them and set about cleaning up the house. Hikaru helped Sachiko. The occasional weak tremor froze them in their tracks, but as each one died down, they gritted their teeth and got on with the job again. Hikaru remained calm and steady. His parents were grateful to Tamon for being at his side.

Dinner was boiled pasta with instant sauce, cooked on a portable gas stove. The water had come from a neighbor with a well. The simple meal tasted wonderful. Hikaru's smile returned.

When darkness fell, they lit a lantern. Like anybody who had gone through the disasters of 2011, the Uchimuras had a stock of emergency equipment and supplies. There was nothing to lose by being prepared. Five years ago, however, few had been prepared.

"I was scared, but it wasn't like last time," Sachiko said while cleaning up from dinner. "It makes a huge difference just to have a house still standing."

"Sure does. And it's a hell of a lot more comfortable sleeping at home than at an evacuation center. Getting pushed and shoved about all night . . . Doesn't look like there's much damage to the fields, either. I'll check them out tomorrow."

"I heard the power will probably be restored tomorrow," Sachiko said.

"Once we have power and water, we can get on with life again. Okay, everybody, let's turn in early and get ready for tomorrow."

"Good idea. I'll put the futons down in the living room, and we can all sleep together. Tamon too."

"Really?" Hikaru sounded pleased.

"Yes. Tamon's one of the family as well. We all sleep together. You won't be afraid then, will you?"

"I'm not afraid of earthquakes."

"That's right. Brave boy. You won't bat an eyelid at any old earthquake."

"What's 'bat an eyelid' mean?" Hikaru asked.

Toru and Sachiko laughed. They explained what it meant while readying the futons, and then they all lay down. This would have been unthinkable last time. Laughing while getting ready for bed in the immediate aftermath of the earthquake.

Toru smiled as he closed his eyes. He was soon overtaken by sleep.

THE FLOOR WAS SHAKING. Toru couldn't tell whether he was dreaming. At the sound of Hikaru screaming, he jumped up. *Earthquake! Bigger than yesterday*, he thought. The walls and supporting pillars of the house creaked and screeched. Toru reached for the lantern he'd put by his pillow, but his fingers found only air. The violent tremors had knocked it over and sent it rolling.

"Toru!" screamed Sachiko.

The tremors knocked Toru from his feet. He fell down onto the futon, landing on his backside. "Sachiko, where's the flashlight? I can't find the lantern."

Sachiko flicked on the flashlight. The beam showed swirls of dust falling from the ceiling and pillars swaying like waves. The groans of their house's wood frame filled their ears.

"Toru!" Sachiko screamed again. The next moment, the ceiling collapsed. Hikaru's screams mingled with Sachiko's.

Toru flung himself flat. His fingers brushed against snapped pillars, and he choked on the dust. Sachiko grabbed hold of his right arm and gripped it tightly. Still, the tremor continued, and debris continued to rain down on their heads.

Toru's eyes searched for Hikaru. He saw him crouched down, hands covering his head, and Tamon standing poised by his side. It must have been terrifying for a dog, too, but Toru saw no fear in Tamon. Only determination to protect Hikaru.

Toru dragged himself to his feet. An earsplitting noise filled the air, and as the floor began tilting, Toru fell down again. Their eighty-year-old home could no longer withstand the onslaught of the earthquake. It had begun to break apart.

"Hikaru!" Toru reached toward him while flat on his back.

A pile of debris from the ceiling was starting to accumulate in the middle of the living room. The floor sloped toward the mound. Hikaru and Tamon were at the back of the room, on the other side of the pile, with walls on three sides and no window. The path was completely blocked. To get to Hikaru, Toru needed to get around the debris.

The tremors had begun to subside. But the house was making an unearthly rasping noise.

"Don't move, Hikaru. Tamon, look after Hikaru." Toru lifted himself off the ground and took a step in Hikaru and Tamon's direction.

"Hikaru!" Sachiko screamed as the south wall began collapsing inward. At the same time, the roof caved in.

"Hikaru!" Toru cried out.

The roof came crashing down at the same moment the wall crumbled onto Hikaru and Tamon. Tamon threw himself across Hikaru's body. It was the last Toru saw of them.

6

t's a real shame."

The voice came from behind as Toru stood staring, stunned, at the ruins of the old house that had once been their home. It was Tanahashi. He was dressed in work clothes and tall boots with a towel wrapped around his neck. Tanahashi's house had partially collapsed, and he was busy cleaning up.

"You, too, Tanahashi . . ."

"But you went through the Great East Japan earthquake. To think ya moved down here only to have the same thing—"

"No point holding a grudge against nature," Toru replied. It was strange, but he really didn't feel bitter about his family's run of bad luck.

"Is that the remains of the dog?" Tanahashi pointed his jaw at the urn in Toru's hands.

"Yes." Toru had gone to the crematorium as soon as it opened. He had just returned from picking up the ashes. "He protected Hikaru. He was a fine dog." Toru gave a faint smile.

"He certainly was a fine dog."

The fire department had reached them about an hour after the quake subsided. In the meantime, Sachiko and Toru had kept talking to Hikaru from outside. Hikaru was alive. He had responded to their voices. But he was pinned down and unable to move. Tamon was with him, so he wasn't afraid, he told his parents.

When the firefighters arrived, they began clearing away the rubble in the dark. After an hour, Hikaru and Tamon were rescued from the ruined house. By some miracle, Hikaru was unharmed. Tamon had protected him and survived too. But he had been injured, his body pierced by a splinter of wood from a ceiling beam.

Sachiko went to the hospital with Hikaru in the ambulance, while Toru loaded Tamon into the mini truck and headed for the vet. The road was blocked in numerous places, and he was forced to make many detours along the way. He finally arrived, only to be told that an operation was impossible because there was no power.

"It'd be the same everywhere. And even if you did manage to find a clinic with power, it would take too long to get there."

Dr. Maeda examined Tamon using a flashlight.

"He's probably got internal damage. He'll be in pain. Shall I make it easier for him?"

Toru didn't grasp what Dr. Maeda was saying.

"Euthanasia. I think it's the best we can do for him."

"I . . ."

Toru touched Tamon as he lay on the examination bench. His body, usually brimming with strength, was weak and trembling.

"Does it hurt, Tamon?" Toru asked. Tamon opened his eyes and looked at him. "Hikaru's fine. Not a scratch on him, because of you."

Tamon closed his eyes. Even in his weakened state, Hikaru was in his thoughts.

Toru stroked Tamon gently on his head. "Please do it," he said.

Once the words had passed his lips, a powerful wave of grief surged up from deep in his breast. He wept as he watched Dr. Maeda send Tamon on his journey to heaven.

"Thank you, Tamon. I'm so sorry."

Tamon's eyes opened once more. He looked at Toru. Then he closed his eyes and did not open them again.

Toru laid Tamon's motionless body on the passenger seat of the truck. Dr. Maeda had wrapped him in a clean white sheet. It was the least he could do, he said.

Toru sighed repeatedly as he drove. Should he tell Hikaru that Tamon was dead? Hikaru was finally recovering from the trauma of the last quake. Hearing that Tamon was dead was bound to give him another shock. Would he retreat back into his own world again?

Nevertheless, Toru knew he couldn't keep the truth from

him forever. Hikaru would ask where Tamon was, and he would have to tell him. He would not lie to his son. When Hikaru was born, he and Sachiko had decided that they would never lie to him.

When Toru reached the hospital, he woke Sachiko, and together they went out into the corridor. Toru told her that Tamon was dead. Sachiko dropped to the floor in a crouch and stifled her sobs. After a while, she said she wanted to say goodbye to Tamon. They left the building and walked across the parking lot to the truck. On the way, Sachiko took hold of Toru's hand. Gently he squeezed it back.

Sachiko touched Tamon. "Thank you," she whispered.

"He was thinking about Hikaru even in his last moments," Toru told her.

"They had a special bond. Tamon protected him to the end. He really was Hikaru's guardian angel. Sent by the gods."

"What do we tell Hikaru?"

"We have to tell him the truth. No lies—isn't that what we said?"

"What happens if the shock makes him revert?"

"He'll be all right—Tamon's with him." Sachiko's voice rang with deep conviction.

"But, Sachiko—"

"This is Tamon we're talking about. Just because he's dead doesn't mean he's abandoned Hikaru."

Her words lifted a weight from Toru's chest. "You're right. That's just like Tamon. Even when dead, he'll be at Hikaru's side. Protecting him forever."

"That's right. That's our Tamon."

Sachiko touched Tamon one more time and sniffled.

HIKARU POLISHED OFF his breakfast. His appetite had not suffered, nor was there a single scratch on him. It was a miracle, the doctor had said. Toru didn't tell him it was thanks to Tamon. It was enough for the family to know of Tamon's devotion and sacrifice.

"Hikaru, I have something to tell you," Toru said after breakfast, when Hikaru was itching to get up.

"What?"

"It's about Tamon."

He could see Sachiko's shoulders tense up as she stood by the bed. Sachiko was praying. *Please, Tamon, protect Hikaru.*

"What about him?"

Toru also prayed. *Please, Tamon. Protect Hikaru.*

"Tamon protected you. Did you know that?"

Hikaru nodded.

"You were both trapped under the wall, and Tamon was badly injured. He died."

Hikaru blinked many times.

"He's not with us anymore."

"No, Dad. Not true." Hikaru spoke in a clear voice.

"What?"

"Tamon here. Inside." Hikaru pointed to his own chest. "Tamon talk to me. He says, 'Don't worry, Hikaru. You're okay. I with you always. Don't worry.'"

Toru and Sachiko looked at each other. Sachiko's eyes filled with tears. Hikaru had never spoken at such length before.

"Tamon dead, not gone, Dad."

"Yes, I suppose you're right."

"I'm sad I can't hug him. But it's okay. I can feel him. Here. Next to me now. Can't you feel him, Dad? Mom?" Hikaru turned to look at Sachiko.

"I do. Tamon's here with us now."

"Yes." Hikaru smiled.

Sachiko also smiled, quietly through her tears. She could almost see Tamon sitting on the floor, looking up at them joyfully.

"I love Tamon," Hikaru said.

"Tamon loves you too." Toru took his son's hand and nodded.

"SO, WHADDAYA PLAN ON doing now?"

The sound of Tanahashi's voice brought Toru back to the present.

"I don't know how much government assistance will be available, but we plan to try to start over again here."

"Well now, glad to hear it. There's so many of us old folks around here, and not many homes with children anymore. With young Hikaru around and doing fine, we will have to do our best too."

Toru knew that the senior citizens in the village were aware that Hikaru wasn't like normal children and that they cared about him, but nobody had ever said as much.

"It did Hikaru a power of good, that dog turning up. He started talking and running around the place."

"He certainly did."

"It was a pleasure to see. That dog didn't just cheer up Hikaru, but all us old folks as well. It's a real shame he died. Is Hikaru doing all right?"

"He's doing fine. Even though Tamon's dead, it seems he's still alive in Hikaru's heart."

"You don't say. Well, I'm glad to hear it." Tanahashi smiled.

The wind blew, sending small ripples across the surface of the rice paddies. Toru felt he could almost see Tamon running across the water.

few months later, Toru received a message on social media.

Dear Mr. Uchimura,

Please excuse this message from out of the blue. The other day I saw your post about a dog called Tamon. My younger brother kept that dog for a short time. I saw the photograph, and I am sure of it. He has the same eyes, with a strong, determined look. Plus it's a mix of German shepherd and some kind of Japanese breed. My brother also called the dog Tamon. Five years ago he died in an accident, and Tamon disappeared. If you would like to know more, please let me know.

The sender's name was given as Mayumi Nakagaki. She lived in Sendai. Toru set about writing a reply to her.